THE CITIES
AND THE FEDERAL SYSTEM

AMERICAN FEDERALISM
The Urban Dimension

This is a volume in the Arno Press collection

Advisory Editors
Robert M. Fogelson
Lawrence E. Susskind

Editorial Board
Bernard Frieden
Richard P. Nathan

*See last pages of this volume
for a complete list of titles.*

The Cities and
the Federal System

ROSCOE C. MARTIN

ARNO PRESS

A New York Times Company

New York / 1978

Editorial Supervision: JOSEPH CELLINI

———◆———

Reprint Edition 1978 by Arno Press Inc.

Copyright © 1965 by Atherton Press

Reprinted by permission of the Aldine
Publishing Company

Reprinted from a copy in the University
of Illinois Library

AMERICAN FEDERALISM: THE URBAN DIMENSION
ISBN for complete set: 0-405-10474-X
See last pages of this volume for titles.

Manufactured in the United States of America

———◆———

Library of Congress Cataloging in Publication Data

Martin, Roscoe Coleman, 1903-1972.
    The cities and the Federal system.

    (American federalism)
    Reprint of the ed. published by Atherton Press, New
York.
    Includes bibliographical references and index.
    1. Federal government--United States. 2. Federal-
city relations--United States. 3. Intergovernmental
fiscal relations--United States. 4. Grants-in-aid--
United States. 5. Metropolitan areas--United States.
I. Title. II. Series.
[JK325.M37 1977]   353   77-74949
ISBN 0-405-10495-2

The Cities and
the Federal System

ROSCOE C. MARTIN
Syracuse University

The Cities and the Federal System

Atherton Press
New York

Preface

The emergence of America as a metro-urban society has had profound consequences for every phase of national life, but nowhere have its effects been greater than in the domain of government. The growth of the city and its evolution into the metro-city has cast up problems more complex and intense than any previously known. These have come to command the concern and resources of all governments, federal as well as state and local; for as they have gained general attention they have emerged as national problems.

Coincident with national involvement in problems once held to be local has come a rise in federal government relations with the cities. Such relations, though in fact of long standing, have increased greatly in number and intensity since 1933. The result is a significant expansion in the practice of federalism, one marked by the emergence of the cities as partners in the federal system. This volume treats of the expanded federal partnership, and argues that it is not only a fact but a fact to be welcomed.

Alexis de Tocqueville spoke of ". . . the good sense and practical judgment of the Americans . . . in the ingenious devices by which they elude the numberless difficulties resulting from their federal constitution." The development explored here reflects the federal system in its process of constant but evolutionary growth, revealing it once more as a flexible arrangement capable of adjusting to new demands without serious shock or violence. De Tocqueville would have expected American federalism to adapt without undue wrench to the new and pressing needs of the emerging metro-society. This it has done—or is doing.

v

The obligations incurred in the preparation of this volume are many. The Social Science Research Council supported my research through a Senior Research Award in American Governmental Affairs. Syracuse University not only gave the leave of absence necessitated by acceptance of the Award, but subsequently added a semester's sabbatical leave which made it possible for me to concentrate on concluding the project. I desire particularly to express my thanks for the grant and leave which made the study feasible in the first place.

A great many federal officials extended hospitality and lent assistance during repeated (and sometimes protracted) visits in Washington. In particular, the executives of the Federal Aviation Agency, the Public Housing Administration, and the Urban Renewal Administration cooperated to make it possible for me to work extensively in the records of those agencies. The officials of the Advisory Commission on Intergovernmental Relations likewise rendered material assistance. So also did the heads of various professional and quasi-professional associations, who welcomed me at a number of national and regional meetings where I was able to interview many local officials—mayors, urban renewal, public housing, and airport directors, planning officials, and members of appropriate boards and commissions. My research carried me pretty well all over the country. Notably I spent two to three weeks each in study in Denver, Norfolk, Philadelphia, and Syracuse. Everywhere I was extended every courtesy and given all possible assistance. Finally, a number of academic colleagues discussed with me the problems which inevitably arose as the study progressed, and Professor Charles R. Adrian read the manuscript in its entirety and made suggestions which resulted in its material improvement.

For assistance rendered along the way I am profoundly grateful. The many contributors did what they could, but it was not given to them, nor to all of us together, to produce a study beyond criticism. The book doubtless has technical flaws; if so, they are mine. It presents and argues a point of view which is by no means universally accepted. The interpretation, too, is my own.

Syracuse, New York   Roscoe C. Martin
Summer 1965

Contents

Tables

1.

A Nation of Cities

It will hardly come as news that America latterly has emerged as an urban society, with the city as its characteristic feature. The process of transformation from rural to urban has covered many years, and it has been the subject of recurrent comment over the last four decades. Thirty years ago the National Resources Committee appointed an Urbanism Committee, whose report called attention in striking fashion to the developing trend.[1] More recently the Department of Agriculture, which most people would identify as the citadel of rural America, took poignant note of the growth of the cities by inquiring what metropolitanism means for rural dwellers.[2]

Notwithstanding what may be presumed to be general familiarity with the trend toward urbanism, it will prove useful to examine the highlights of that trend, and more particularly some of its major consequences. It is the thesis of this chapter that the urbanization of the nation has resulted in a new society, which in turn has produced problems of a scope and intensity, and indeed of a kind, not previously known.

---

[1] *Our Cities: Their Role in the National Economy,* Report of the Urbanism Committee to the National Resources Committee (Washington, D.C.: United States Government Printing Office, 1937).

[2] United States Department of Agriculture, "The Stake of Rural People in Metropolitan Government" (Economic Research Service, Miscellaneous Publication No. 869, Washington, D.C., 1961).

1

THE URBANIZATION OF AMERICA

Americans are not without reason in the pride they take in their country's pioneer heritage. The America of colonial days was in truth a frontier society, notwithstanding occasional pockets of genteel living along the seaboard. The achievements of the formative years of the Republic were those of pioneers, whose intellectual talents should not be allowed to obscure the fact that they were essentially sons of the soil. In 1790 the young country's population was 95 per cent rural, only 5 per cent urban. New York, with not quite 50,000 people, was far and away the largest city; Philadelphia, with less than 30,000, was a distant second. The "bold yeomanry" dwelled in the villages and on the farms of the tidewater and in the inland settlements.

Never again was the ratio of rural to urban dwellers to be so favorable for those who prefer the country way of life, for each decennial census since 1790 has shown a smaller proportion of the total population to be rural and a larger proportion to be urban. In only one decade (1810–1820), indeed, has the percentage increase in rural growth exceeded that in urban. The cities gained the ascendancy in 1920, when for the first time the urban population exceeded the rural. Since that time the gap between the two has widened continuously. The period 1950–1960 illustrates the trend: during that decade, the urban population increased more than three times as fast as did the rural population. Table 1 provides a summary of the trend in the urban-rural ratio since 1790.

The trend toward urbanism has been characterized by two separate but related phases. The first was marked by the rise of the cities. In 1790 only New York and Philadelphia had populations of 25,000 or more; in 1960 there were 676 such cities. In 1790, the largest city (New York) had somewhat fewer than 50,000 people; in 1960, there were 332 cities each with a population of 50,000 or more, and these cities contained nearly 65,000,000 people, or 35 per cent of the country's total. In 1850 only New York had more than 500,000 people; in 1960, 21 cities had 500,000 or more and 51 had 250,000 or more. In 1850 the fiftieth largest city had fewer than 15,000 people; in 1960 the fiftieth largest had almost 262,000 people.

Table 1. Changes in the Urban-Rural Ratio, 1790–1960

Year	Per Cent	
	Urban	Rural
1790	5.1	94.9
1810	7.3	92.7
1830	8.8	91.2
1850	15.3	84.7
1870	25.7	74.3
1890	35.1	64.9
1910	45.7	54.3
1930	56.2	43.8
1950	64.0	36.0
1960	69.9	30.1

From 1890 to 1930 the number of places with 2,500 and more people increased from 1,417 to 3,165; from 1930 to 1960 there was a further increase to 4,699.

In 1850 no city had as many as a million people; in 1960 the five cities of a million or more had about 17 million people. Of these five cities, only two were in existence in 1790. The two, New York and Philadelphia, had a combined population of about 78,000. In 1960 the combined population of these two cities had grown to almost 10 million. Of the remaining cities of one million or more, Chicago (second in size) appeared first in the census of 1840, which recorded for the youthful city a population of less than 5,000. Los Angeles, now third in size, appeared first in the census of 1850 with a population of 1,610. Detroit, now fifth, was recorded first in 1820 when its population was listed as 1,422. In 1960 the five largest cities had a combined population approaching 10 per cent of the nation's total.

For well over a hundred years urban growth centered in the cities, and particularly in the larger cities. As long ago as 1920, however, a subtle but unmistakable change in the growth pattern began to assert itself: a rapid increase in population began to be experienced in the territory surrounding the larger cities. The new growth was in the suburbs, whose people were independent of,

4 The Cities and the Federal System

though in many ways closely associated with, the neighboring central city. To this agglomeration of central city plus suburban fringe the term "metropolis" came to be applied. The Census Bureau called these concentrations metropolitan districts, and subsequently standard metropolitan areas and later still, for the census of 1960, standard metropolitan statistical areas (SMSAs). However denominated, the metropolitan area (metropolis) encompassed a central or parent city together with its suburban communities, some incorporated as municipalities, some not. The principal feature of the new era was the rapid growth of the suburbs by comparison with their central cities.

If Phase 1 of the history of urban growth was characterized by the rise of the city, Phase 2 is featured by the emergence of the

Table 2. Percentage Growth in Population of Standard Metropolitan Areas by Decades, 1900–1960

	Per Cent Increase by Decades					
Area	1900–1910	1910–1920	1920–1930	1930–1940	1940–1950	1950–1960
United States Total	21.0	14.9	16.1	7.2	14.5	18.5
Standard Metropolitan Areas	32.0	25.4	27.1	8.5	21.8	26.4
Central Cities	36.6	27.7	23.8	5.4	13.9	10.7
Suburban Rings	24.3	21.3	33.2	13.9	34.7	48.6

Source: Roscoe C. Martin, *Government and the Suburban School* (Syracuse, N.Y.: Syracuse University Press, 1962, volume 2 in *The Economics and Politics of Public Education* series), p. 11. Reproduced by permission of Syracuse University Press. For the problems encountered in constructing the table, see this reference.

metropolis. Urbanization was the hallmark of the first period, suburbanization that of the second. The census of 1920 constitutes a rough, but in no wise exact, dividing line between the two.

Table 2 provides a general indication of the nature of metropolitan growth. The table reveals that the metropolitan areas have outgained the United States as a whole in population growth in every census since 1900, in all save one decade by a substantial margin. It also discloses that the central cities grew more rapidly than did their suburbs to 1920, but from that year forward the suburban rings took command of metropolitan population growth. From 1930 on suburban growth has always been close to three times that of the central city, and from 1950 to 1960 it was more than four times as great. The growth has been fastest in the rings surrounding the larger cities: from 1950 to 1960 the five largest cities increased only one per cent, their suburbs 71 per cent. By 1960 no more than 51.4 per cent of the metropolitan population resided in the central cities; almost half, therefore, had found residence outside, a large percentage of them in the suburban communities. It is quite clear, then, that the suburbs are the principal beneficiaries of the nation's expanding population. Suburbanization is indeed the overwhelming feature of the prevailing trend in population growth.

Lest suburban growth obscure the larger significance of the metropolis, it will prove useful to list a few facts that suggest the importance of these major concentrations. In 1960 the continental United States had 212 metropolitan areas. These areas covered 10 per cent of the country's total area, but contained 63 per cent of the population. From 1950 to 1960 the metropolitan population increased by 26.4 per cent, that of the rest of the country by 7.1 per cent. Population growth was greatest in the areas ranging from 500,000 to 1,000,000 in population; the increase was 36 per cent. There was growth, however, all along the line, for only 8 of the 212 metropolitan areas failed to gain in population from 1950 to 1960. Population density in the metropolitan areas in 1960 was 364 per square mile, and this ranged from 5,336 per square mile for the central cities to 183 for the ring areas. Population density for the country as a whole was 51 per square mile.

The metropolitan areas in 1962 had 51 per cent of the *number* of properties assessed for local general property taxation but more than 72 per cent of the assessed *value*. The metropolitan areas also contained 20 per cent of the nation's total number of governments, but these governments employed almost 65 per cent of all full-time local government personnel.

The census reports are loaded with data that indicate the dominance of the metropolis in American life, but perhaps enough has been said to suggest its significance. It is a growing significance, and there is every likelihood that it will increase rather than diminish in future years. As a single indicator, the metropolitan areas increased in population considerably more rapidly from 1950 to 1960 than they did between 1940 and 1950. Current census estimates indicate that the metropolitan trend continues to run: from 1960 to 1962, the average annual growth for the fifteen largest metropolitan areas was 1.2 per cent. This suggests a moderate slackening off from the frantic growth rate of the last decade, but the decrease is not great. There are no signs to indicate that the role of the metropolis will not become even more dominant, or that the suburban rings will not continue to grow more rapidly than other segments of the population. What do these trends mean for American society?

EMERGENCE OF A NEW SOCIETY

William Cowper's fatuity that "God made the country, and man made the town" finds counterpart in America in the myth that all good things come from the land. In a 1964 Fourth-of-July sermon, a rural preacher in an upstate New York village proclaimed that the good life is not to be found in the cities. He summarized the time-honored national view, still widely prevalent, of the respective values of the countryside and city in the nation's life. It will be argued in this section that the rural life of song and story has undergone so many drastic modifications over so many years that it is no longer realistic to speak of rural America as America; instead, an urban society, evolving gradually over the course of something like a century, has now come to the point where it not only can but also must affirm its unique character and its claim to special attention. It is not asserted that country and city embrace totally different values, for in such fields as war, peace, and foreign aid there is indeed a mutuality of concern. There is, moreover, an interdependence, although it is heavily weighted in the direction of substantial and increasing independence for the city. For all this, the interests and values of country and city are substantially dissimilar, and these dissimilarities grow sharper with the passing of time. There is emerging, perhaps indeed there *has emerged,* a new metropolitan society to whose needs many of the institutions and values rooting in a rural past are almost wholly inadequate. Let us examine some relevant data to see how this society has developed and what it is like.

The Country and the City. Farm residence offers the interesting paradox that while more and more people live on farms, fewer and fewer seek to make a living there. Thus the rural nonfarm population increases while the rural farm population diminishes, as it has for many years—from 30 per cent of the total population in 1920 to less than 8 per cent in 1962. From 1950 to 1960, farmers and farm managers decreased more than 43 per cent and farm laborers and farm foremen almost 39 per cent. At the same time the number of farms decreased sharply: from more than 6 million in 1940 to 3.7 million in 1959. This is, of course, not all loss; for though farms have decreased in number of recent years, they have increased in size—from an average acreage of 216 in 1950 to an average of 303 in 1959. And as farms have grown in size, the value of their products, of farm lands and buildings, and of farm implements and machinery likewise have increased. With the increase in the size of farms and the appreciation of their capital equipment has gone a substantial improvement in the farm operator level-of-living index. In absolute terms, then, the residents of the farms who remain farmers are not doing badly. Judged by the nostalgic standards appropriate to the rural America of another day, indeed, they may well be considered to have succeeded in their quest for the "good life," particularly when it is remembered that the level-of-living index takes account of such amenities as electricity, telephones, home freezers, and automobiles.

By criteria which permit measurement of growth, however, the countryside fares ill by comparison with the city. Construction of farm residential and service buildings was at a virtual standstill from 1950 to 1959, while residential nonfarm construction increased more than 58 per cent, industrial construction almost 98 per cent, and the construction of office buildings and warehouses 368 per cent. To employ a different kind of criterion, during the decade ending with 1960, housing units increased 34 per cent inside the standard metropolitan statistical areas, only 15.5 per cent outside. During the same decade agriculture, forestry, and fisheries increased their contributions to the gross national product only a little more than 13 per cent; at the same time the percentage increase for manufacturing was more than 35, that for wholesale and retail trade 27, and that for public utilities 138. As a percentage of those employed, agricultural workers decreased almost 50 per cent from 1940 to 1960, whereas workers in manufacturing enterprises increased 64 per cent and those engaged in construction almost 83 per cent. The comparative sluggishness of economic activity on the farms reflected itself in low individual earnings: the median income for the male urban worker in 1960 was $4,532, that for the male farm worker $2,098.

In the abstract, then, rural America may afford its devotees a satisfactory means of livelihood; in comparative terms, however, it is clear that agriculture has not begun to keep pace with the growth registered by other segments of the nation's economy. The statistics authenticate the impression one may glean from casual observation —rural life is in sharp decline, substantially all growth occurs in the urban areas.

Urban Dwellers and Farm Folk. The device most commonly employed to compare the characteristics of city and country life is the urban-rural classification. These are, however, gross categories, each containing more than one subdivision. Urban territory comprises all communities of 2,500 and up, whether incorporated or not; this of course includes as major components the larger (central) cities and the suburban fringes. The rural population in turn may be divided into those who reside on farms and those who do not: "rural farm" and "rural nonfarm" are the terms employed by the Census Bureau. There are therefore shadings within each major category. The central city represents the extreme in urban-ness, the rural farm the extreme in rurality. The suburban and the rural nonfarm subcategories usually fall between the two extremes by the customary measures of urbanism and ruralism. We shall employ varying (though hopefully consistent) terminology here, depending upon the categories for which relevant data are available.

The thesis to be developed is that urban dwellers and farm folk differ from each other in so many fundamental ways as to make of them quite distinct kinds of people. The husbandman symbolizes the bucolic America of an earlier day; he and his way of life are all that is left of rural America and the traditions that went with it. For his part, urban man stands for the new America, for a twentieth-century society molded by the twin forces of urbanism and industrialism. The traditions and myths, the stereotypes, the habits of thought and action, the provincialism, and the attitude toward the rest of the world which characterized those who practiced agrarianism as a way of life—all these are scarcely relevant to the problems of urban America.

An important difference between farm folk and urban dwellers concerns national origin. More than 90 per cent of all farm residents were born of native parentage, as compared with only 77 per cent of urban residents. On the other hand, 16 per cent of all urbanites were born of foreign or mixed parentage and almost 7 per cent were foreign-born; the companion figures for the farmer are 8 and less than 2 per cent respectively. The melting-pot function, at one time more generally shared throughout the nation, lately has been taken on almost entirely by the cities. That their people are less bound to the land, more volatile, more given to social experimentation, and less suspicious of public action is not a matter for wonder. Nor is the presence of contrary qualities throughout much of rural America. Stability, satisfaction with things as they are, orthodoxy, conservatism: these are the hallmarks of a rural society. The mobility which marks modern America—almost 20 per cent of all Americans move at least once a year—is a concomitant of urban rather than of rural life. Almost 30 per cent of all native urbanites were born in a different state from the one in which they now reside, as compared with only 12 per cent of farm dwellers. Some 37 per cent of city folk have lived in their present dwelling for only a matter of two years, for farmers the figure is 21 per cent. Three times as many farm folk as urban dwellers have always lived in the house they now occupy. The conclusion to be drawn from these figures is clear: farmers like it where they are, and they stay put; city dwellers, on the other hand, move frequently.

Orthodoxy finds reflection in church affiliation. The rural population comprises only 30 per cent of the total, but more than 43 per cent of all Protestants are found in rural areas. Roman Catholics are urban residents by a majority of almost 4 to 1; among Jews, the preference for the city over the country is 24 to 1. The significance of these disparities in distribution in such fields as education and politics is very great.

Family size provides yet another criterion for contrasting farm and city dwellers. Within the metropolitan areas (as defined by the Census Bureau), the population per household in 1960 was 3.23, outside the metropolitan areas it was 3.39. As is almost always the case, the extremes were to be found in the central cities, where the family size was 3.05, and the rural farm areas, where it was 3.78. With respect to age, the central cities dominate at both extremes of the distribution curve. Almost 11 per cent of their total population is under five years in age, as compared with somewhat less than 10 per cent for the rural farm population. At the other end of the scale, almost 10 per cent of the population of the cities is over sixty-five years of age; the companion figure for farm folk is somewhat more than 9 per cent. The difference here is not great, but it is substantial. It is clear that the cities have more very young and more old people than the rural areas have.

The urban dweller is much better educated, in terms of formal schooling at least, than his rural counterpart. Among white city dwellers, the median years of school completed by persons twenty-five and over in 1960 was 11.5; among farm people, the comparable figure was a little less than 9. Moreover, city dwellers are taking care that the gap shall not be closed: in 1960 more than 5 per cent of all urban residents between twenty-five and thirty-four years in age were enrolled in school as against less than 3 per cent for the farm population. The figures for ages five and six likewise are significant: among those in the city, more than 69 per cent were enrolled in school in 1960; for farm children of the same age range, the percentage enrolled was 48. Between six and eighteen years of age the differences between city and farm folk in school enrollment are not great, but beginning with the eighteenth year a spread in percentage enrolled asserts itself and becomes progressively greater with each succeeding age group. It is clear that city youth enroll earlier and remain in school longer than do their rural counterparts. The significance of this fact, in terms of the resulting urban demands for special education programs, will not be lost.

Of the total urban population, 57 per cent were in the labor force in 1960 as compared with less than 52 per cent of the farm population. For women over fourteen in the labor force, the comparative figures were much more striking: they were, for urban women, more than 37 per cent, for farm women a little less than 23 per cent. Thus the labor force contains a considerably larger percentage of urban workers than of rural workers; in particular, a much larger percentage of urban than of rural women finds it prudent (or necessary) to work.

The results obtained for their labors are strikingly different for city and country workers. Fewer than 4 per cent of urban families had incomes of under $1,000 in 1960, whereas well over 15 per cent of farm families had such incomes. At the other extreme, almost 18 percent of all urban families had incomes in excess of $10,000, as compared with less than 7 per cent of the farm families. As noted earlier, the median income for male urban workers in 1960 was $4,532, that for male farm workers $2,098. In terms of income, therefore, the contrast between city and country is sharp and painful.

The role of the Negro in urban society is worthy of special mention. The Negro population, long overwhelmingly rural, is migrating with accelerating speed to the cities. In 1950 the urban-rural ratio among the Negro people was approximately 62:38, but by 1960 the Negro population was 74 per cent urban, only 26 per cent rural. For purposes of comparison, it may be observed that the white population in 1960 was almost 70 per cent urban, about 30 per cent rural. The industrial cities of the northeast and the midwest are the principal goals of this vast migration.[3] The city, particularly the large city, has become the Mecca for the Negro refugee. He may

[3] It should be noted that, notwithstanding the Negro flood to the cities, Negroes still constitute only a small minority of the urban population in general. This is not true, however, of individual cities: Washington, D.C., for example, is now more than half Negro in population.

not fare any better in his new urban environment than he did on the farm, but at least, he tells himself, he will have a chance to do better.

The increasing concentration of Negroes in the cities has the effect of emphasizing the extremes. Thus the Negro family is considerably larger than the white family in the city. (It is also larger—much larger—in the farm areas.) Nonwhites (principally Negroes) are much more poorly educated than are the whites: the median years of school completed by white urban dwellers twenty-five and over are 11.5; the comparable figure for nonwhites is 8.7. In terms of income, there were more than three times as many nonwhite as white families that made under $1,000 in 1960, and only a little more than one-fourth as many that made $10,000 and over. The median income for nonwhite male workers in 1960 was only a little more than half that of the white workers.

The Negro therefore fares ill in his new abode when compared with the white. When his urban lot is compared with that which he knew on the farm, however, it is seen that he does substantially better in the city. His family, though large, is smaller than it was on the farm; his education, though scant, is better than before; and his income is close to four times as high as it was. There seems little reason to doubt that, over time, the city will put its stamp on the Negro dweller as it has on the white. In the meantime, the flood of undereducated, unskilled Negroes to the cities, principally from southern rural areas, vastly complicates the governmental, political, social, and economic problems of urban society.

Here, then, is the way urban America looks when compared with the vestigial rural society of an earlier day. In terms of racial origins, mobility, religious affiliation, inherent personal attributes, outlook on life, education, school enrollment, composition of the labor force, income, and color composition the urban dwellers of industrial America are so completely different from their agrarian counterparts as to constitute virtually a new and radically different people. Business as usual is a strange precept for an urban/industrial America, particularly when it is remembered that the public institutions and the procedures they employ were designed for a dying agrarian society.

The differences between residents of the central city and those of the suburban fringe, although not so striking as those between urban and rural residents, nevertheless are significant. This has led some observers to reject the urban-rural dichotomy in favor of a more precise classification. This may be necessary for scientific analysis, although for present purposes the gross categories "urban" and "rural" would appear adequate. Certain it is that the differences between the urban and the rural, particularly the rural farm, populations are greater than those between city residents and suburbanites.

Some observers speak of the homogenization of the American people, pointing out that, as the urban component of the total population increases, urban characteristics will tend more and more to prevail throughout the nation. Thus as the urban population approaches 100 per cent of the total, the social and economic characteristics of all the people will come to resemble more and more closely those of the urban dwellers. The end will come when the nation has become one great mega-city; then all Americans will look and act like urbanites, for all will in truth be urban dwellers.

Notwithstanding the city has placed its stamp indelibly on American culture, that time would appear to be some decades away. Physical and institutional metropolization are quite different things, as observation of legislative behavior in many a state will attest. Traditions long held, ways of thought, patterns of action and reaction may be expected to be modified in deference to the fact of urbanism only partially, grudgingly, and over many years. Meanwhile those who reside in the cities live and work and think and act in ways which set them apart from those who live on the land. They represent the vital, experimenting, growing edge of American society. Simply by living and working in large and complex agglomerations in an industrial, scientific age, they generate problems that are without precedent in American history.

SOME CONSEQUENT PROBLEMS

The problems consequent on America's metamorphosis into an urban society stem largely from the number, kind, distribution, and way of life of the cities' people. The central consideration here, an overwhelming one, concerns sheer numbers. The nation had just short of 180 million people in 1960; within four years that number had increased to more than 190 million (a growth of 6.2 per cent), and estimates for 1985 vary from 248 to 276 million, depending on assumptions regarding future fertility. From 1950 to 1960 some 84 per cent of the total population growth took place in the metropolitan areas, and there is no reason to suppose that there will be any marked change in the growth ratio of 5 or 6 to 1 in favor of the urban areas. The nation has seen its urban population grow at the expense of its rural for more than 170 years; it is altogether likely that the ratio will further widen, though possibly at a diminishing rate. Apart from numbers alone, features of the urban population which give rise to new and special problems concern the extremes in age (under five, over sixty-five) that characterize core-city dwellers, their high degree of mobility, their manner of life, and their workways—all mentioned earlier, albeit briefly. Relevant too is the change in racial composition, marked chiefly by the unprecedented in-migration of the Negroes, now in process. Let us examine briefly the major problems that flow from the concentration of 63 per cent of the nation's population in 10 per cent of its area.

Among the many urgent urban problems in want of attention, six have been selected for consideration here. Each is characteristic of and in its more virulent form is peculiar to an urban society. Each grows from the concentration of large masses of people in small areas. Each in its current incarnation is *sui generis,* for none has congruent precedent in American history.

First among the problems virtually unique to an urban society is the physical blight that besets the center of the city. Many of America's cities are old by New World standards. Center-city structures in general are likely to be forty to fifty years old, and many buildings were constructed a hundred years ago or more. Because there has never been any systematic effort at renewal, much of the downtown area of the typical city is obsolescent. Obsolescence takes the form of a downward spiral, with business and residential property, in want of renovation or repair, falling to less-than-desirable occupants, and undesirable occupancy in turn leading to further deterioration. One sees frequent reference to the cities' blighted areas. Where such areas are residential, they come to be characterized as slums. Blighted areas and slums are by no means limited to the large cities, but the form of the problem and its pervasiveness there cause the widespread obsolescence of the city to be regarded as a peculiarly urban malady.

Companion to the problem of downtown decadence is that of substandard housing. In city after city dwelling places adequate in their day have fallen prey to the downward spiral. Substantial homes that are within walking distance of the business district are devoted to a lesser use when the original owners die or move to the suburbs, and presently they come to house two or three or more families instead of one; or perhaps they are converted to third-rate rooming houses or "hotels." With the departure of the single-family owner, such a house begins to fall into disrepair and obsolescence sets in. The result of this process, multiplied thousands of times over, is the inferior housing that initially characterizes the slum. Cheap rooming houses and tenements in time make their own contributions, and presently full-fledged slum conditions come to prevail in the area fanning out from the business district. A large percentage of the population of any major city will be found to occupy substandard housing, and this is particularly true of the economically marginal and racial minority groups. Like blight in general, submarginal housing is by no means limited to the larger cities; but also like blight it is particularly and peculiarly characteristic of such cities. Slums and slum dwellers are in truth among the most ubiquitous of all the manifestations of an urban society.

The urban transportation problem assumes many forms, among which the mass movement of travelers within the city and the transit of commuters to and from the suburbs are the best known and most widely discussed. In part the problem arises from sheer volume, illustrated, for example, by the facts that 33 per cent of the suburban labor force work in the central cities, and 64 per cent of all workers travel to their jobs by private car or car pool while another 12 per cent travel by railroad, elevated train, subway, bus, or streetcar. In part the problem arises from the growing number and use of automobiles. That this problem will increase in complexity is suggested by the estimate that autos will increase in number 40 per cent from 1960 to 1970. The Metropolitan Planning Commission of Atlanta recently forecast that by 1970 that city, in the absence of a rapid transit system, would need 120 expressway lanes radiating from downtown, along with a 28-lane central city connector. Such demands make of transportation a prime space problem, and so call up the entire issue of land-use planning. A different aspect of the problem, one often overlooked, stems from the important part played by the cities in air transportation. The current emphasis on recreation likewise creates new issues. Transportation is as pervasive a problem as any faced by the city; it is explicitly both a prime product and a prime problem of an urban society.

Education is at the same time an urgent national problem and one with unusual urban overtones. Three aspects of the problem may be mentioned by way of suggesting its nature. First is the inescapable and ever present pressure generated by increasing numbers: school enrollment increased 17 per cent from 1958 to 1963, and most of these new students sought accommodation in urban schools. Second, the extremes in ages of urban students (under five and over eighteen), along with the demands for technical training, create a need for special education facilities not experienced elsewhere. The rural areas may make do with a standard curriculum administered over the customary age span, but the cities cannot. Third is the complexity of racial integration in the cities. The impact of desegregation on the South, rural as well as urban, will continue to draw the headlines, but the problem of devising and administering an integrated school system in the city is no less complicated. Moreover, it is a distinctively urban problem.

Yet another problem consequent on the concentration of large numbers of people in small areas concerns water and air pollution. Polluted water has long been recognized as a major cause of disease: outbreaks of cholera in the cities of the eastern seaboard, notably Philadelphia and New York, a century and a half ago focused attention on the problem and led to remedial measures. The measures taken were inadequate, however, and the problem of a pure water supply remains to this day a matter of urgency in most cities. More recently air pollution has come to be recognized as a kindred if not (as yet) as an equally urgent problem. Water and air pollution are two of the most pressing problems confronting the modern city. As before, they are problems preponderantly resultant from the conditions of urban life.

A condition of the gravest import has to do with the pathological patterns of behavior which attend modern life. Notable is the problem of juvenile delinquency, which appears to be more prevalent in the city, particularly the large city, than in the rural areas. In 1961 nearly 14 per cent of all urban persons arrested for aggravated assault were under eighteen years of age; the corresponding figure for rural areas was just over 9 per cent. Comparable figures for robbery were 23 and 14 per cent, for larceny 50 and 34 per cent, for auto theft 61 and 51 per cent. There are several possible explanations for these figures; but the inescapable fact is that, for whatever reasons, urban youths violate the law more often than rural youths do. Country youngsters commit acts of personal violence and steal automobiles too, but not in such numbers as the juveniles of the city.

The problems of modern society summarized here are overwhelmingly *public* in nature, impact, and consequence. They are public also in that they are dependent upon public instruments for their solution—or, since ultimate solutions are illusory, for their amelioration. The import for governments of problems consequent on rapid urban growth is strikingly summarized in a recent publication of the World Health Organization, which concluded, "Every increment of 1,000 metropolitan residents in the United States necessitates *additions* of 4.8 elementary school rooms and 3.6 high school rooms, 100,000 gallons of water, 1.8 policemen and 1.5 new firemen, 8.8 acres of land for schools and recreation areas, one hospital bed, and a fraction of a jail cell."[4] Private enterprise has a role, sometimes an important one, to play in some areas; but generally speaking the problems of metro-America are problems of government. This brings us to brief consideration of government in relation to urban problems.

[4] Reported in *Metropolitan Area Problems: News and Digest,* a publication of the Graduate School of Public Affairs, State University of New York, vol. VII, no. 5 (September–October 1964), p. 7.

The new society possesses one pre-eminent feature that makes it unique in American experience—traditional thinking about the division of governmental responsibilities has but limited relevance to the problems it generates. In their origin these problems were for the most part "local," that is, municipal, and for decades the focus of attention by those concerned about them was the city itself. More recently it has come to be recognized that concentration on the municipality will no longer suffice, because the problems most in want of attention long ago overran local boundaries. For perhaps three decades it has not made sense to leave responsibility for these problems where accident deposited it more than a century ago.

An urgent issue of our time centers on the parts to be played by the several levels of government in the new metro-society. The continued concern of the cities may be taken for granted, for they are at the very eye of the hurricane; yet the cities have amply demonstrated that, acting alone, they lack the capacity for metro-governance. The states have a traditional responsibility for the cities and their problems, but few would maintain that they have discharged that responsibility in anything approaching satisfactory fashion. The federal government reveals both a growing awareness of metro-urban problems and a willingness to bring national resources to bear in seeking their abatement, though it remains to be seen what results federal participation will produce.

It may be argued persuasively that no one government is equal to the challenge of the metropolitan age, but that on the contrary all must contribute to the effort if the problems identified here, and others like them, are to be effectively addressed. The question is no longer whether the federal government shall take a hand in an area reserved by tradition to the states and, more particularly, the communities, but rather how it can contribute most effectively to the common effort. The problems requiring urgent action may not be dismissed, nor may responsibility for them be longer evaded, by calling them local responsibilities. These are problems not of the cities alone but of the American people, and their alleviation requires nothing less than concerted action by all governments. The problems of the metro-city, in short, have been elevated to the national stage; they require national action. President Johnson clearly and explicitly recognized this fact in his "Message on the Cities" to the Congress of the United States of March 2, 1965.

This is a study of the respective roles of the three governments—federal, state, municipal—in seeking solutions to the worsening problems of urbanism. Stated another way, it is a study of the vertical relationships among governments in the broad domain of metro-urban affairs. Of recent years the national government has actively joined in the search for means to alleviate urban ills. It is the study's central thesis that the resulting relationships between the federal government and the cities, which have increased sharply over the last three decades, have wrought significant changes in the federal system. This is, then, basically a study in the operational aspects of American federalism.

2.

The American System:
The Many and the One

Where should responsibility for the great new metro-problems be placed? The answer will be neither easy nor clear-cut. Tradition suggests one course of action, which expediency seconds; but necessity may require another. The route indicated by necessity—that is, by the urgent need for *all* governments to take vigorous, positive action respecting the problems at hand—has important implications for the practice of federalism. Our search therefore may properly begin with an inquiry into the federal system.

What is intended here is not a disquisition on federalism but an examination of the federal system in the context of federal-state-city relations. The central theme will be the capacity of the federal system to adapt to changing conditions, and particularly its flexibility in the face of new problems. The legal and philosophical aspects of federalism have been developed expertly and often elsewhere. Our concern here is a special one: the federal system in operation. Our focus will be on intergovernmental relations within the federal structure.

THE FEDERAL SYSTEM

A discussion of the American federal system which aspires to realism must begin with an understanding that local government was here first. The governments with which the colonists were first

21

acquainted were the towns—local, home-grown, rural units close to the people. The colonial governments came next, the products equally of domestic recognition of the need for a unifying agency and of a companion but separate decision by a distant sovereign. The commonwealths were long establishing a stable base, and they spoke with an uncertain voice right up to the time when the issue of independence was resolved. The localities retreated slowly and grudgingly before this unifying trend, for even the watery prestate governments of colonial days were tolerated without enthusiasm. To this day, indeed, the state and its government are regarded with suspicion in some quarters; Vermont, for example, is considered by its citizens to be a confederation of towns, and its state government is treated accordingly. It was from this stony soil that the Union grew.

Even so the need for a central government of some description became increasingly manifest. In the early efforts at union and the discussions that enveloped them, however, the question was never how much local autonomy should be preserved. For the colonies/ states and their communities had a monopoly of *all* autonomy at the moment of independence. The problem rather turned on the minimum concession of power essential for the maintenance of a shadow union. Local rights and privileges, and in particular the privilege of freedom from government, was a hard-won and dearly-held possession. Freedom and diversity were virtues ingrained and, where threatened, fiercely defended; union was only a necessity.

But if there must be some form of union, the colonies, and in their turn the states, might elect any of several choices. The easiest alternative, the one fraught with least danger to local independence, was confederation. Little more than an alliance among sovereign bodies, the confederate form of union had been tried and found wanting. The government under the Articles of Confederation answered this description, in both form and outcome. At the other extreme was a unitary arrangement featured by a strong central government and relatively weak member units. The founders of the Union saw little in history to justify the expectation that a unitary system would satisfy the wants of their freedom-minded constituents. Prominent in the debates which attended these considerations was the tug of war between diversity and unity, between experienced anarchy and feared paralysis, between local independence and national power.

The solution, as every schoolboy knows, was a compromise called a federal system. Standing on a middle ground between the two extremes, the federal system sought to secure the best of both worlds. It recognized the validity of two constitutionally-secured levels of government, one an anterior level comprising the thirteen states, the other a derivative level consisting of the national or central government. The keynote of the federal system is the condition of equilibrium that prevails between the two levels. A moderate shift in power in either direction would upset the equilibrium, resulting in deterioration into a confederation in one direction or into a unitary system in the other. The central problem of a federal system is the maintenance among its members of this essential balance, which from its very nature is delicate and uneasy. The middle way is nowhere harder to travel than in a federal system.

The federal planners, assembled in national convention, sought to secure the necessary balance through a written constitution, itself as much an innovation as the federal system it proclaimed. The troublesome problem of distribution of powers was dealt with by delegating certain specific powers to the natonial government and reserving those not delegated to the states. Section 8 of Article I is a listing of the powers vested in Congress. Ten amendments to the Constitution were adopted almost immediately as a "Bill of Rights." Amendments IX and X contain the following significant wording by way of more explicit reservation of powers and rights:

> ARTICLE IX. The enumeration in the Constitution, of certain rights, shall not be construed to deny or disparage others retained by the people.

> ARTICLE X. The powers not delegated to the United States by the Constitution, nor prohibited by it to the States, are reserved to the States respectively, or to the people.

Other clauses as well sought to secure and preserve the desired state of equilibrium, but the doctrine of delegated and reserved powers constituted the keystone of the federal arch.

But if the Constitution was explicit in some areas it was tentative, even inconclusive, in others. In experience, it turned out to be in fact a quite flexible document. The Constitution is celebrated for its terseness; it was kept brief because to have been definite on all points at issue would have been to invite controversy and to encourage dissent. Partly by design and partly through necessity, therefore, the key concepts and clauses of the Constitution required interpretation from the very beginning.

This was true first because the basic concept of a federal system, the distribution of the powers of government between the central government and the constituent members, is not subject to a once-and-for-all disposition. The wall between the states and the nation was not impermeable, nor from the nature of things could it have been made so. The powers of government in their totality were not any more susceptible of detailed listing in 1787 than they are today; hence the division of powers between the two levels was not (nor was it regarded as) ironclad. The inexact nature of the distribution was recognized in Section 8 of Article I, which ended on the note that Congress shall have the power "to make all laws which shall be necessary and proper for carrying into Execution the foregoing Powers, and all other Powers vested by this Constitution in the Government of the United States, or in any Department or Officer thereof." This is the celebrated "implied powers" clause, under which Congress has extended its legislative power into fields unknown to the framers of the Constitution. It is perhaps the one clause above all others through which the Constitution has been kept current over more than 175 years. That the constitutional listing of powers was incomplete and in a sense tentative was further recognized explicitly in the Tenth Amendment, quoted above.

Apart from the slippery nature of its central concept, the Constitution was replete with words and clauses that required interpretation, both on the spot and recurrently in the light of unfolding experience. There was, for example, the power to "lay and collect Taxes, Duties, Imposts and Excises, to pay the Debts and provide for the common Defence and General Welfare of the United States . . ." (Article I, Section 8). What is a tax, on what objects may it be laid, for what purposes, in what amount? And what does the "General Welfare" comprehend? Another illustration is found in the power vested in Congress to "regulate Commerce with foreign Nations, and among the several States, . . ." The powers to lay and collect taxes, to provide for the common defense and general welfare, and to regulate commerce have been subject to necessary interpretation from the beginning of American constitutional history; and these are only three, albeit three of the most important, of the many grants and prohibitions requiring interpretation. Such phrases are the repository of the Constitution's vaunted flexibility, which has made it possible to adapt an eighteenth-century document to the uses and needs of a twentieth-century world.

The other side of the coin of flexibility reads doubt and uncertainty—uncertainty primarily concerning the distribution of powers between the states and the nation. The Constitution's phrasing in the early days gave comfort both to those who would interpret that document strictly so as to secure the widest possible range of powers to the states and to those who would give it a loose or liberal construction so as to allow the maximum of power to the national government. These were identified presently as antifederalists and federalists, and subsequently as advocates of states' rights and champions of the national union. The issue will be recognized at once as the continuing contest between local autonomy and centralization. The tortured history of the controversy eventuated in a Civil War appeal to arms, taken on the specific question of the right of the states to secede from the union. The slavery issue provided the immediate occasion for the conflict, but the fundamental question concerned the nature of the union.

The lasting lesson of Appomattox is that the American system is a federal one; it is, as the Supreme Court has put it, "an indestructible Union, composed of indestructible States." Neither government is judged to be paramount over the other except with respect to a very few well-defined areas. The consequential areas in which one government may take action without reference to the other therefore are limited. The American system is in truth a partnership in which the doctrine of dual federalism, held generally for upward of a century and still widely embraced, has in fact given way before the practice of cooperative federalism. The latter concept will be examined with some care later; it is mentioned here merely to suggest the spirit of American federalism as it has long been practiced. It remains a flexible, open-ended, evolving system. The Civil War attested its toughness, as the long history of American constitutionalism has repeatedly witnessed both its adaptability and its resilience. The last and least thing that could be said of America's federal system is that it is fixed, formal, and certain in its distribution of powers and in the relations between its partners. On the contrary, it remains to this day an experimental system, one which probes constantly for pragmatic accommodation where legal principle fails. It is above all a practical system, in 1965 application as in 1790 concept.

What the federal system means at any given time will be an aggregate of what it has been held to mean with respect to major but individual current issues. There are many decision centers through which the direction of American federalism is determined. The Presidency is one such, and it is altogether proper to speak of the Roosevelt administration as one under which the national government flowered, of the Eisenhower administration as one which sought to promote the role of the states. Another decision center is the Congress, though by reason of the emergence of the President as a national leader its role is generally held to be a declining one. Another yet is the Supreme Court, which when all is said and done is the final, though by no means unlimited, arbiter of federal issues.

In the early post-Civil War period a combination of weak or indifferent presidents and a conservative court led to a failure to consolidate the gains of the union. Thus many issues that might have been settled in favor of the national government were resolved instead in favor of the states. States' rights, temporarily sidetracked, came to be reasserted, in some quarters with even greater fervor than before, so that one was justified in wondering whether the cardinal lesson of the Civil War had not been lost after all.

For all the hesitancy of the early postwar years, however, the tendency has been toward a stronger and more active national government. This has been particularly true during the twentieth century. The trend can be followed generally through the history of the Presidency; for a strong chief executive almost uniformly brings on increased national activity, a weak or complaisant one renewed emphasis on the states. Thus a Roosevelt was followed by a Taft, a Wilson by a Harding-Coolidge, a Roosevelt-Truman by an Eisenhower, an Eisenhower by a Kennedy-Johnson. The swing from centralization to decentralization and back is by no means constant, but the over-all trend is clearly discernible.

Notwithstanding President Eisenhower's distrust of the national government and his announced intention of "returning" their "rightful" powers to the states, the Supreme Court in the early 1950s took an opposite view of contemporary needs. To the Warren Court there were problems which required adjustment, which the states had chosen and clearly meant to continue to ignore, and which the national government had the legal power to deal with. These convictions led to a series of decisions, beginning in 1954, which some critics have characterized as a constitutional revolution. By treating such major issues as civil rights and legislative apportionment, the court did in fact bring within the domain of national responsibility areas previously left largely to the states. Through both presidential and, perhaps more important, Supreme Court leadership, therefore, the current trend reinforces the secular tendency toward increasing emphasis on national action.

An important by-product of this trend is the renascence of the perennial controversy between states' righters and nationalists; for this feud, never far below the surface, waxes and wanes with the spirit of the times. In a larger sense, this was the lasting significance of the 1964 campaign for the Presidency. President Johnson would not wish to be called a nationalist, yet his policies and programs called for national action in the face of the failure of the states to act. And whatever the label accorded him, none could take him to be an advocate of states' rights in the current meaning of that term. Senator Goldwater by contrast embraced states' rights joyously. He would have placed much greater reliance on the states for action even in areas of national concern—in the field of civil rights, as a single example. In an important sense, the campaign turned on the nature of the federal system. Its outcome confirmed once again the decision in favor of the union symbolized by Appomattox Court House.

What is the posture of the federal system in 1965? Three things may be said by way of summary. First, the importance of the role of the national government has been authoritatively reaffirmed. No stronger than circumstances warrant, it is nevertheless as powerful as conditions require. This is in substantial part the meaning of the civil rights battle of Selma, Alabama. The nation is ascendant. Second, the states, rebuffed in the states' rights drive which presumed to speak for them, nevertheless remain basic partners in the federal system. The lesson of the Supreme Court "revolution" is that the nation is no longer dependent solely upon ineffective or recalcitrant states for the achievement of national policy. The states enjoy rights and powers, both through constitutional provision and through practice, which permit them to play as important a role in the governance of America as they may wish to play. That some states do not conceive their role as an active and vigorous one is a matter of state, not of national, decision. The states generally— though by no means all states—are recumbent; whatever their potential role as partners in the federal system, many states are neither minded nor equipped to take vigorous action with respect to large affairs. Third, the federal system remains the flexible, evolving, vigorous instrument it has been from the beginning. Once again it has demonstrated its adaptiveness, its ability to accommodate to the requirements of changing times and new conditions.

THE PLACE OF THE CITIES

We turn now to an examination of the role of the cities in the American system of government. As before, the purpose is a limited one. Aspects of the problem which would be vital in another context are passed over here in favor of emphasis on the position of the cities with respect first to the states, second to the nation. In this domain there are wide and frequent gaps between theory and practice, hence it will be necessary to emphasize operational arrangements as well as legal framework.

The Cities and the States. The spirit of local independence ran high in America at the time of the Revolution, as indeed it does to this day. The hard-won fruits of rebellion were considered to be local gains, and any enterprise not associated with the immediate community was regarded with suspicion. Government in particular was held close to the bosom of the people. They had won the right to control their own affairs, which to the greatest degree possible were to be vested in the seeable, touchable government of the small community.

If we consider the sacredness attached to individual freedom and by easy transfer to close-at-home government, it is not surprising that local government early came to enjoy a certain sanctity in the popular esteem. Nor is it a matter for wonder that a legal doctrine was conjured up to buttress little government. The transition from confidence and satisfaction in local institutions to veneration of them was natural; the next step was somewhat more difficult, but it, too, was taken in time. It led to the enunciation and broad acceptance of the doctrine of the inherent right of local self-government.

This doctrine, evolved early as a local counterweight to the centralizing tendencies set in motion by the new state governments, enjoyed wide support during the first decades of the Republic. In coldly practical terms, its acceptance in law would have resulted in local government anarchy for the new nation. It was rejected in favor of the doctrine of state supremacy vis-à-vis its local governments. It is worthy of note that this rejection signaled a reversal of the teachings of colonial history; for by it the anterior governments, the local communities, were made secondary and the derivative governments, the states, became primary.

The local governments, and particularly the growing cities, were loath to accept this metamorphosis, and they continued sporadically to assert their prior rights and privileges with respect to local affairs. Three-quarters of a century passed before the ghost of inherent local rights was authoritatively laid to rest. This was accomplished by the Supreme Court of Iowa, which in 1868 incorporated the following passage in a historic decision:

> Municipal corporations owe their origin to, and derive their powers and rights wholly from, the legislature. It breathes into them the breath of life, without which they cannot exist. As it creates, so may it destroy. If it may destroy, it may abridge and control. Unless there

is some constitutional limitation on the right, the legislature might, by a single act, if we can suppose it capable of so great a folly and so great a wrong, sweep from existence all the municipal corporations in the State and the *corporation* could not prevent it. We know of no limitation on this right so far as the corporations themselves are concerned. They are, so to phrase it, the mere *tenants at will* of the legislature.[1]

The decision of the Iowa court was subsequently upheld by the Supreme Court of the United States. It continues, however, to be known as Dillon's Rule, after the Iowa justice who originally decided the case and wrote the preceding passage.

Dillon's Rule has been tested many times by cities seeking loopholes or limitations in it, but it continues as the ruling principle governing the legal status of the cities. Barring a state constitutional grant or guarantee (a contingency covered by the rule as originally stated), the city has no rights apart from or above those granted by state law. Legally it is a creature of and is utterly dependent on the state. Harking back to the alternatives available to the framers of the Constitution in 1787, the state is therefore unitary rather than federal in structure in the eyes of the law.

But practice often departs from law, either by blinking legal dogma or by modifying it in application. Nowhere is this aphorism better illustrated than in the position of the city vis-à-vis the state. The law has it that the city is the creature of the state, but practice accords the city a considerable measure of independence. One factor which mitigates the harshness of the legal rule resides in the persistence of tradition; for the ghost laid to rest by Judge Dillon almost a century ago appears recurrently to set forth its case and plead its cause. The right of local self-government is among the hardiest of American traditions.

Above the sense of outrage at any infringement of local autonomy is the fact that the state itself has moved to grant its cities certain basic rights. The principal (but not the sole) vehicle by which such a grant is conveyed is "home rule," a device by which the state concedes to its cities (or counties) more or less autonomy

[1] *City of Clinton v. Cedar Rapids and Missouri River Railroad Company,* 24 Iowa 455 (1868); quotation at p. 475.

over local affairs. The device varies in nature and scope; its extreme form is found in the grant of power to the city to draft and adopt its own charter. Home-rule rights may be spelled out in either constitutional provision or statutory law, and may be either broad or limited. The constitution of Missouri since 1875 has contained a provision giving the cities wide latitude with respect to the adoption and amendment of their charters. Other states granting their cities a broad measure of home rule are California, Michigan, and Texas. To date, about half of the states have placed in their constitutions provisions giving their cities home-rule powers over charter formation and change. Cities in many states therefore enjoy a measure of autonomy through home rule.

Nor is the political strength inherent in the city to be overlooked. Again sheer numbers are on the side of the cities, and will be increasingly so; for if almost 70 per cent of the nation's people reside in the cities, then two-thirds or more of the voters, actual or potential, likewise reside there. Political control of the state by the cities is widely suspected; in 1964 the Republican candidate for governor of Illinois charged that the Democratic incumbent owed his election to and was indeed the tool of the Chicago Democratic machine. Any candidate for statewide office in New York must make his peace early with New York City; it has been more than forty years since New York has had a governor who was not a resident of or at least not closely identified with its largest city. In any election where sheer number of votes is controlling, the influence of the cities is great and undoubtedly will increase in the future.

A development in immediate prospect concerns the impending reapportionment of state legislatures. Reapportionment, if and when achieved, in itself will produce no millennium, although in time it will make the legislatures more representative and in turn will produce a legislative body more attuned both to urban needs and to current issues. In further consequence it will mitigate the time drag in dealing with urban problems. The cities are destined to play an increasingly important role in the affairs of the states, in considerable part because of legislative reapportionment.

Organizations of cities and city officials likewise provide the cities with instruments for the wielding of political influence. The league of cities and the association of mayors will almost always command a respectful hearing at the state house. Even the legislature, which because of the apportionment system has not had cause to fear the strength of the cities in the past, listens to the spokesmen of these organizations with more than ordinary respect. The cities of course do not speak with one voice, for differences do exist—between New York City and the upstate New York urban centers, as an example. Nevertheless they have little difficulty uniting to resist state assaults on urban prerogatives. Local differences are set aside in the face of a common enemy.

The cities are not nearly so supine as Judge Dillon's statement would lead us to believe. Something quite like a federal system has grown up within the states; for while the law calls for state supremacy, practice has produced a considerable measure of municipal autonomy. As a matter of law, the states could of course modify this system in any way they might see fit, but in point of fact they would find it difficult to abridge any important right enjoyed by the cities. Now and again a state takes punitive action against a city (usually one governed by the political party not in control of the state house), but such occurrences are so rare and the storm they provoke so violent as simply to underline the significant change which practice has brought about in the Dillon Rule: *de jure* the state is supreme, *de facto* the cities enjoy considerable autonomy. The intrastate federal system rests largely upon custom fortified by statutory law, but it is none the less stable for that. Custom provides a strong foundation for most institutional practices, while a body of legislative law which is not subject to repeal and which can be amended only with the concurrence of its subjects affords almost as firm a base as the constitution itself.

The Cities and the Nation. There is a general disposition for observers to dismiss the subject of the place of the cities in the federal system with the brisk conclusion that cities are not members of the federal partnership. In a technical sense this is true, for the Constitution of the United States nowhere accords recognition to local governments. In operational terms, however, the situation is quite different, for the cities have played a significant part in the functioning of the federal system for many years. This has prompted one student of the subject to observe, "Local governments—rural, urban, and suburban—are part and parcel of the American federal system."[2] The author argues that the practice of cooperative federalism has long since brought the cities—indeed, all local governments—within the orbit of the federal system notwithstanding explicit recognition was withheld by the framers of the Constitution. Thus they have been accorded *de facto* recognition as members of the federal partnership, though denied constitutional status.

The quasi-federal system that exists within the states is concrete and persuasive evidence that the position of the cities is considerably stronger than the law lets on. There are also certain recent and current developments—the mass of the urban population, the number and size of the cities, and the velocity of urban government—that point to significant strengthening in the position of the cities. It will be remembered that in 1960 there were 332 cities with 50,000 or more people, and that these cities contained 35 per cent of the nation's total population. In that same year the five largest cities (a million or more each) had a total population of some 17.5 million, approximately 10 per cent of the country's total. Chicago had 35 per cent of all the people in Illinois, New York City more than 46 per cent of the total population of New York State. In the states containing the five largest cities, the proportion of the population residing in metropolitan areas ran from 73 per cent (Michigan) to almost 87 per cent (California).

By other measures also the larger cities in particular make their influence felt in their several states. In 1961 Chicago contained 30 per cent of Illinois' total assessed value of property subject to local general property taxation; the comparable figure for New York City was 61 per cent. As in the case of population, the larger metropolitan areas dominated the assessed property values of their states. For the states containing the five largest cities, the proportion of assessed values lying within the metropolitan areas ran from some-

[2] Daniel J. Elazar, "Local Government in Intergovernmental Perspective," in *Illinois Local Government,* a publication of the Institute of Government of the University of Illinois, *University of Illinois Bulletin,* vol. 58 (May 1961), p. 24.

what less than 74 per cent (Illinois) to 91 per cent (New York). In public employment, New York City had well over twice as many employees as New York State, Chicago had almost two-thirds as many as Illinois, and Detroit had close to half as many as Michigan.

The importance of the cities is likewise reflected in the role they play in the national economy. In terms of expenditures, indebtedness, and services performed—in terms, that is, of the criteria used to measure economic activity—that role is increasingly influential. Whether they thrive or languish is a matter of first importance to the nation. No longer can the national government permit the economies of the cities to run at idling speed, for the national economy tends increasingly to reflect the aggregate of the urban economies.[3]

In yet another direction the cities play a role of national importance. In the distant past urban governments served almost exclusively urban needs, fulfilling the traditional role of local units in the American system of government. Then came the states, then the nation, to utilize existing governments with their established organizations and procedures. Today much of the activity of the city reflects the demands of state and national programs, for the vigorous practice of cooperative federalism has made of the cities in significant part handmaidens to higher governments. In many important action areas the cities have become instruments of national policy through service as administrators of national programs.

In Chapter 1 half a dozen of the more urgent metro-problem areas were examined briefly, and the conclusion was reached that these problems require resources of an order and kind not commanded by state and local governments. With respect to such problems it is fruitless to debate what is urban, what is state, and what is national, for they represent a confluence of concern by all governments. This fact has been recognized at the national level, where many programs—in the fields of public housing, urban renewal, and water quality management, to name but three—have been launched

[3] A. A. Berle, Jr., has argued this point persuasively in an article entitled "Reflections on Financing Governmental Functions of the Metropolis," *Proceedings of the Academy of Political Science,* vol. XXVII, no. 1 (May 1960), pp. 66–79.

with an eye to the alleviation of these urban-national problems. President Johnson, taking note of the convergence of national and urban concerns, not only has promised further vigorous action by the government in Washington but also has taken positive steps to implement that promise.

Other concerns than that of the cities are of course relevant to this discussion. One is that of the states, whose interest in urban problems and capacity for dealing with them will be appraised in the next chapter. Another is that of the national government, which in some respects is closer to the cities than the states themselves. In contemplating the stake of the nation in the cities, and more particularly the future course of federal-city relations, three factors suggest themselves as worthy of special consideration. First is the increasing political strength of the city. National holders of elective office are not likely readily to forget—nor to be allowed to forget— the needs of the cities. Second are significant current modifications in the practice of federalism in the face of long-standing and in some areas serious shortcomings in governmental performance. In *An American Dilemma,* Gunnar Myrdal was generous in his appraisal of the American Dream, but there is growing public dissatisfaction with the gap that separates what we profess from what we do, what could be from what is. Third is the rapid and continued increase in the nation's wealth, which reflects itself in mounting resources available for the support of public programs. These factors point toward the nationalization of problems previously held to be urban and toward increased reliance on the cities as active participants in their administration. This is not the place to argue the case for direct access by the cities to the national government, but it is not premature to suggest that there are currents in being which bid fair to work important changes in the traditional relations among the three levels of government in the American system.

QUEST FOR OPERATIONAL EFFECTIVENESS

The search for workable arrangements—that is, for adaptations which would translate legal forms into structures and procedures adequate to meet operational needs—has followed two major lines.

The first has produced a maze of governmental units which in 1962 numbered 91,236; by census definition all of these except the nation and the fifty states are local governments. They are, of course, central to an analysis of the subject of governmental adaptation to program requirements, but they are not of immediate relevance to the study at hand. Of greater concern is the second line of search, which relates to the amplification of the federal system.

In broad outline, the nature of the American system was generally understood by 1875. The Civil War had determined the union to be a federal one, while the Dillon Rule had declared the cities subject in all fundamental particulars to their respective states. The basic partners in the American system therefore were the nation and the states. Even if we omit mention of what the Constitution neglected to say, it seems reasonably clear in what it did say regarding the respective powers of the two. The list of powers conferred upon the national government appeared adequate to foreseeable needs, while the residual powers seemed to make the states a bottomless repository of authority over all things else. Although it was never contemplated by those who conceived the federal system that the nation and the states would pursue completely separate and distinct courses, a judicial doctrine resting essentially upon that concept had gained almost universal currency. It resided in the notion of dual federalism, summarized by Chief Justice Roger B. Taney in 1858 in these words:

> And the powers of the General Government, and of the State, although both exist and are exercised within the same territorial limits, are yet separate and distinct sovereignties, acting separately and independently of each other, within their respective spheres.[4]

This concept of federalism, which, though at its height perhaps a century ago, has been embraced throughout most of our national history, appeared the more logical by reason of the seemingly clearcut division of powers in the Constitution.[5]

[4] *Ableman v. Booth,* 21 Howard 506 (1858); quotation at p. 516.
[5] The literature of federalism is vast, learned, diverse, and in some part illogical and contradictory. The Workshop in American Federalism of the University of Chicago, under the leadership of the late Professor Morton Grodzins, has produced a number of studies which suggest a fairly drastic

As legal doctrine dual federalism enjoyed general acceptance over the course of many years; but as a description of the federal system in operation it came to be recognized as artificial. The notion of two parallel streams of government, one labeled state, the other national, with little or no crossover from one to the other, simply was not in accord with the way the federal system operated. Some reserved powers were discovered to gain in significance if shared by the states with the central government, whereas the latter found itself the beneficiary of state collaboration in many areas in which it enjoyed delegated powers. There was, moreover, the broad sea of concurrent powers—powers that might be exercised by either state or nation, or both. With respect to concurrent powers in particular, the states and the central government frequently found themselves in a position of interdependence, with each profiting by turn from the collaboration of the other.

The concept of dual federalism appears scarcely adequate to describe the network of interrelations that grew up between the two major federal partners. "Cooperative federalism" would seem a more apt term. This phrase has gained wide currency during the last quarter-century, in reference particularly to the "new federalism" of the New Deal.[6] It signifies the common sharing of public responsibilities by two or more "levels" of government. The sharing may be national-with-state (or the reverse), national-with-state-with-local, state-with-local (though technically this is an intrastate rather than a federal matter), or federal-with-local. The Tennessee Valley Authority, which through a network of "agreements of co-operation" has brought literally scores of governments together in collaborative action in the Tennessee Valley, is a prime exemplar of cooperative federalism. Cooperative federalism describes a confused,

revision of our thinking about the nature of federalism. In particular, these studies question sharply the applicability of the doctrine of dual federalism throughout much of our history. On Professor Grodzins' nomination and my invitation, Professor Daniel J. Elazar, a former member of the Workshop, prepared a memorandum for my use in this study. I found this memorandum useful, though it goes without saying that Professor Elazar is not to be taxed with responsibility for what I have said here.

[6] See especially Jane Perry Clark, *The Rise of a New Federalism* (New York: Columbia University Press, 1938).

even a chaotic, arrangement, and it has to recommend it initially only the fact that it also describes operating relations among the governments—relations that have existed since the early days of the Republic. As a concept it lacks the neatness of the notion of dual federalism, but it has the advantage of a foundation in reality.

Cooperative federalism has been shown by Elazar to have prevailed from the early 1800s in such areas as "the extension of internal improvements, the maintenance of a sound nationwide fiscal system, the establishment of appropriate educational facilities, and, to a more limited extent, the provision of necessary public welfare aids." He mentio..s the joint stock company and the cooperative survey as two of the major means by which cooperation among governments was achieved in the early days, and illuminates numerous cases of inter-level cooperation achieved by these (and other) means.[7]

As practiced throughout the nineteenth century, cooperative federalism possessed certain characteristic features. First, it rested upon a common concern among governments in public programs of wide significance. A program which through generality of interest might be considered national but at the same time was possessed of immediate state or local importance or had a direct and demonstrable local impact was the natural starting point for an agreement among governments to share responsibility. Second, intergovernmental cooperation served, in the nineteenth century as now, as a device for matching resources with needs. In important program areas the only resources available were those of the general government, whereas the needs frequently were quite particular. Third, the instrument most commonly employed for encouraging and implementing cooperative arrangements was the grant-in-aid. Throughout the last century the grant was usually in land; with the substantial depletion of the public domain shortly after the beginning of this century, money grants came into vogue. The central government possessed

---

[7] Daniel J. Elazar, "Federal-State Collaboration in the Nineteenth Century United States," an unpublished paper prepared for delivery at the 1962 annual meeting of the American Political Science Association, Washington, D.C. The quotation appears at page 5. For a more extended discussion, see his *The American Partnership* (Chicago: University of Chicago Press, 1962).

all the public land and recently has enjoyed a substantial superiority in the matter of money revenue. It has, therefore, been in a position to act as chief investigator and supporter of cooperative federalism. Fourth, the practice of cooperation has combined national standards with state and local responsibility for administration. This has had the effect of placing a floor under performance without destroying local responsibility for what have been, in impact at least, local problems. Fifth, the setting of standards has entailed a measure of national supervision in the matters both of fiscal management and of achievement of program goals, and this has raised recurrently the question of centralization. These features suggest the nature of cooperative federalism as it has been practiced almost from the beginning of our history.

The participants in these cooperative activities have been identified, by implication at least: they were, first, the national government and the states. It is highly significant, at the same time, that the cities played a not-unimportant role in these cooperative arrangements. The city of Norfolk participated, together with the states of Virginia and North Carolina (and private investors as well), in a joint stock company to implement an Army Engineers plan for the Dismal Swamp Canal as early as 1816; and Hartford benefited from cooperative support for an asylum for the deaf and dumb founded the next year.[8] If the cities were not often singled out as major partners in the practice of cooperative federalism, it was because they were not of much size or separate consequence during most of the nineteenth century and their problems were those common to general local government rather than those of the highly differentiated urban society of today. Because their problems had not yet become specialized, as a rule they were handled in the normal course of dealing with general public issues. Even so, the cities were practicing partners in many cooperative programs from the early 1800s, and in some they were signatories, so to speak, of the agreement on which cooperation rested.

Cooperative federalism has gained wide acceptance of recent years as a term newly popularized to describe the ever increasing practice of cooperation among national, state, and local govern-

[8] Daniel J. Elazar, "Federal-State Collaboration . . .," *op. cit.*, pp. 5, 11.

ments. In point of fact, however, cooperation has characterized the practice of federalism from the early years of the Republic. The Constitution provided for a dual system, but from the beginning dual federalism was more legal myth than operational reality. Clearly the constitutional system required to be energized by a workable set of understandings and arrangements to fill the voids and smooth the harsh edges of legal federalism. The dualism of Justice Taney was transformed into an operationally effective system by cooperative federalism, a device typically American in its pragmatism.

Two observations may be made in conclusion. First, cooperation among different levels of government has been so widely practiced and so well known over the decades as to have gained matter-of-course acceptance. Not much point was made of cooperative federalism in the nineteenth century precisely because it was a universal phenomenon. Second, the question of what government assumes responsibility for action in case of need is of small concern to the citizen. Federal centralization, states' rights, local self-government—these and kindred shibboleths have little significance so long as health programs are run well, streets are fixed, and school is kept. The Federal Council on Intergovernmental Relations demonstrated more than twenty years ago that the citizen's concern is for service defined in terms of answers to felt needs, rather than for legal or ideological justifications. Cooperative federalism is a term which, it may be supposed, lies beyond the vocabulary of the average citizen, but it nevertheless describes the kind of government he is used to. Alexander Pope's much-abused couplet in praise of pragmatism has more relevance here than in most places where it is employed.

AN EVOLVING FEDERALISM

The federal system wherever found is experimental and inexact, whether as concept or as practice. As corollaries it is also flexible, highly adaptive, and ever changing. This is true for example of the federal systems of Canada and Australia, where the relationship between the central government and the states is a matter of constant concern and continuous probing. The federal system was designed to effect a marriage of centrality and diversity; because these concepts (and public understanding of them) vary from country to country and from time to time, there can be nothing static about federalism.

It comes as no surprise that American federalism fits into the common pattern. It is an evolving arrangement for the division of powers and the distribution of responsibilities among governments of different levels. Far from being rigidly bound by philosophical or ideological conceptions, the federal system is a pragmatic scheme that not only permits but also requires adjustments to meet the varying needs of changing times. American federalism, in practice if not in theory, reflects sensitively shifts in presidential leadership, which is chiefly responsible for accelerating or braking adaptation in the system. It is also sensitive to changes in the composition of the Supreme Court, which must be relied upon both for legal interpretations and for legitimating action when it is challenged. The federal system thus reacts positively to change in all its forms—social, economic, political. It is a major instrumentality for adjusting the relations among nation, states, and localities so as to make and keep government in its totality abreast of the needs of the people.

If the federal system is inexact in concept and flexible in practice, it is at the same time possessed of unplumbed depths and untested limits in respect of possibilities for adjustment. When widely felt wants have emerged to command a national consensus on action, ways have been found to meet them. War and depression have produced the most spectacular readjustments in federal-state-local relations, but the modifications introduced all along to make federalism a working reality have been important too. Many modifications of high significance have been introduced under the mantle of cooperative federalism, which in various guises has been engaged in the business of making the federal system operational for at least a century and a half. That federalism will prove equal to future challenges presently unforeseen may be confidently expected; the case of Puerto Rico, recently brought into association with the union as a commonwealth—a status without precedent in either law or practice—is suggestive on this point. It is difficult to believe that American federalism will not prove equal to future demands to be made upon it.

It is significant that, notwithstanding marked modifications in both the law and the practice of federalism, the distinguishing features of the federal system persist in America. Relations among the members of the American partnership are not what they were, or what they were expected to become, in 1800, yet it cannot be truly said that any partner has suffered a loss of fundamental rights or that any has gained in stature at the expense of another. Quite specifically the states, whose leaders now and then complain about latter-day trends, cannot be demonstrated to have forfeited any right to action or to responsibility in any field in which they have had the power and the will to act. If they have on occasion forfeited the right to *inaction*, that is because they have misread the signs of the times or misjudged the conscience of the American people. But that is another story, one more appropriate for telling elsewhere. What is important here is that it be understood that America's federal system has found ways to adapt to new conditions without loss by its partners of any essential rights or prerogatives. The evolution of federalism has been more in practice than in theory; it has reflected pragmatic responses to urgent stimuli rather than abandonment of or modification in fundamental philosophical concepts.

In a commencement address delivered at the University of Michigan on May 22, 1964, President Johnson spoke of the overwhelming problems of the cities in the context of the federal system. These problems, he concluded, "require us to create new concepts of cooperation—a creative federalism—between the National Capital and the leaders of local communities."[9] The ingredients for the creative federalism envisioned by the President are ready at hand. They include principally freedom from commitment to a static doctrine, a fluid concept of federalism, and a willingness to experiment. It does not seem likely that the form of the federal system will be modified in any important way because that does not appear necessary, but the practice of federalism could change significantly in our time.

[9] As reported in *The Washington Post*, May 23, 1964, A6:3.

In contemplating the possible directions and the likely extent of change, we will find it useful to weigh the relative capacities of the partners in federalism against the foreseeable tasks that lie ahead. Let us particularize the question: What are the interests of the national government, the state, and the city in the problems of a metropolitan society? What resources—leadership, vigorous and effective organization, skilled and experienced manpower, demonstrated success in governing, money—is each prepared to plough into the war to make America's cities livable? How deep, how firm, and how effective is any commitment that may be undertaken likely to prove? These are the kinds of questions that are relevant to the President's call for a creative federalism. They are most pertinent and most timely when asked of the states.

3.

Unequal Partners:
The Case of the Reluctant State

The states have achieved a distinctive place in the public forum, for few subjects can be named for discussion that will so swiftly or so surely divide those participating into two opposing camps. To some the state is the bedrock foundation of government, the repository of the bulk of civic virtue and beneficiary of the rest, the one best hope for the maintenance of responsible government and the achievement of public progress in the future. To these advocates, states' rights provides a beacon for the guidance of all who love liberty and detest centralized government. To others, by contrast, the state stands for *status quo* government, one which through failure to adjust to changing conditions has lost touch with real life. Far from offering hope of achieving progress, the state is regarded as a roadblock across the highway that leads to the future. To these observers, states' rights is, to paraphrase, the last refuge of the scoundrel. The debate as to whether the state is hero or villain has been going on for well over a century; if it seems to have developed new insistence and increased shrillness of recent years, the reason may be that we are participating in the argument instead of reading about it.

Our concern is for the states' capacity to function effectively as members of the federal partnership. That they have been less than sensationally successful in coping with the problems of modern society would, perhaps, be generally conceded. The reasons assigned

45

for their shortcomings, however, vary widely. From the Advisory Commission on Intergovernmental Relations (ACIR) we hear that "there has tended to develop a pattern of direct national-local relations in some . . . functional areas which has prevented the States from exercising their rightful role in the Federal system."[1] At the same time there are those who would question this diagnosis, not least because, they would maintain, it mistakes cause for effect. They would argue that the states have not exercised their "rightful role [itself an interesting concept] in the federal system" because of gross deficiencies in the base, organization, and procedures of the state governments. They would argue, moreover, that since these deficiencies are remediable by state action, the states themselves are squarely responsible for their failures to maintain co-equal status in the practice of federalism. The fault, many argue, lies with the states, not with their stars.

The apologists for the states sometimes shift the argument to another base. Thus one who fears big government has stated, "In the final analysis, the argument against the states on *specific* matters must become an argument against federalism *as a whole*."[2] To allow this view is of course to move the focus of the argument from the deficiencies of the states to the viability of the federal system. The contention is a specious one, for it is clear enough that the states suffer from many ailments that in no wise inhere in federalism. This is not to say that the shortcomings of the states and their governments are not reflected in inadequate performance by the states as members in the American partnership, but it is to insist that such deficiencies exist quite apart from the strengths and weaknesses of the federal system as such. That they have important consequences for the federal system goes without saying.

If a federal system, and specifically the American system, is

[1] House of Representatives, Committee on Government Operations, 87th Congress, 1st Session, Committee Print, *Governmental Structure, Organization, and Planning in Metropolitan Areas,* A Report by the Advisory Commission on Intergovernmental Relations, July 1961 (Washington, D.C.: Government Printing Office, 1961), p. 43.

[2] Alfred de Grazia, "Federalism," in *The Conservative Papers* (Garden City, N.Y.: Doubleday and Co., 1964), p. 246.

to function properly all members of the partnership must be strong and vigorous. It is a central conviction of this study that this precondition to success does not now obtain in America in that the states have not been able or willing to assume their share of federal responsibilities, particularly during the last three decades, and that the national government has been compelled to develop active relations with local governments in order to make the American system operationally effective. The point of view embraced here represents an exact and complete inversion of the position taken by the ACIR in the passage quoted above: The states have been unable or unwilling to exercise "their rightful role in the Federal system," *therefore* "there has tended to develop a pattern of direct national-local relations in some . . . functional areas."[3] It is the purpose of this chapter to explore the question why the states have not functioned effectively as members of the American partnership in rising to the challenge of the urban age. The answer will be found in certain palpable deficiencies of the states and their governments.

STATE CONSTITUTIONS

The fifty state constitutions are the basic charters under which the states conduct their affairs. The oldest existing constitution, that of Massachusetts, traces its ancestry back to 1780; the newest, that of Michigan, was adopted as late as 1962. The constitution of Rhode Island is the shortest with 6,650 words, that of Louisiana the longest with 350,000 words. Some qualify as constitutions by a reasonably rigid definition, others are in fact legal codes covering a variety of nonconstitutional subjects, some of them in great detail. In view of the variety that prevails in age, length, and subject matter coverage and treatment, any set of generalizations about state constitutions will be subject to exceptions. Let it be noted early that not every-

[3] The view adopted here accords better with that of the Commission on Intergovernmental Relations which concluded, with respect to the restrictive provisions of many state constitutions, that "These self-imposed constitutional limitations make it difficult for many States to perform all of the services their citizens require, and consequently have frequently been the underlying cause of State and municipal pleas for Federal assistance." The Commission on Intergovernmental Relations, *A Report to the President for Transmittal to the Congress* (June 1955), p. 37.

thing said here applies equally to every constitution. Notwithstanding this caveat, the general drift of state constitutions with respect to the subject at hand is clear enough.[4]

There is no dearth of interest in state constitutions, or of published materials on the subject. For present purposes it will be sufficient to examine four characteristics of the states' basic charter. First, the typical state constitution was drafted to serve the needs and purposes of an agrarian society. Both age and content provide justification for this observation. Twelve constitutions predate the Civil War, an equal number were adopted after 1900. Six constitutions have been adopted since World War II, but another way of saying it is that forty-four are more than twenty years old. Urbanism began to take hold well before 1945, it is true, although the country did not have time to worry much about its consequences until after the war. Agrarianism, however, although declining in statistical terms for many years, remained the dominant influence in most states throughout the years when the bulk of the constitutions were drafted.

Examination of almost any constitution will confirm the overwhelming concern for the farmers on the part of the drafters of the document. Many constitutions accord the agricultural interests special privileges with respect to taxation; not only are certain farm properties—machinery and livestock, for example—exempt from taxation up to a stated value, but also the collection of taxes due is scheduled to suit the farmers' convenience. In California "fruit and nut-bearing trees under the age of four years . . ." are exempt from taxation. In Oklahoma the public schools are required to teach the "elements of agriculture, horticulture, stock-feeding, and domestic science, . . ."[5] Some constitutions enjoin citizens to the observ-

[4] The National Municipal League in 1960 launched a State Constitutional Studies Project which during that year and the next yielded a number of publications of great use and timeliness. The analysis here has drawn heavily on two of these: Robert B. Dishman, *State Constitutions: The Shape of the Document* (1960), and John P. Wheeler, Jr. (ed.), *Salient Issues of Constitutional Revision* (1961).

[5] Robert B. Dishman, *op. cit.*, pp. 16, 17. The point here is not that the tax system was deliberately designed to bestow economic advantage on the farmers, but only that the solicitude manifest in the constitutions reflects a heavy—and persistent—agrarian influence.

ance of frugality, prudence, sobriety and other virtues dear to our rural forebears, often in the language of an earlier day. There is evidence aplenty of the influence of agrarianism on the drafters of state constitutions, for every time one turns a page one stumbles over a milking stool or hears the distant whinny of the plough-mare—but not the cough of the tractor; that came later.

Second, if thirty-eight of the fifty state constitutions were drafted before 1900 and forty-four before World War II, one would seem justified in supposing that the basic charters of the states might be lacking in timeliness. Loss of relevance is not a necessary consequence of age, for even though some fundamental principles are timeless, every constitution contains a provision for amendment. Most constitutions have in fact been amended many times in an effort, in part, to keep abreast of changing conditions. The process of change, however, outruns the best efforts of the amenders; moreover, amendments almost always add, scarcely ever subtract, and less frequently yet revise. The conclusion is warranted that, for all the efforts to keep them abreast of the times, the constitutions are lacking in timeliness; filled with provisions concerning matters that are no longer of concern and neglectful of other matters that are, they seem frequently but little relevant to a world now almost seven decades into the twentieth century.

Third, state constitutions almost uniformly reflect a narrow, restrictive point of view. Because the states are endowed with reserved powers, it has not seemed necessary to enumerate those powers in the state constitution. It has been deemed advisable, however, to circumscribe the state's government in considerable detail, lest in the exploitation of its reservoir of powers it overstep acceptable limits. The constitution thus has come to be regarded as a brake on government rather than as an accelerator, and its repressive function has been stressed at the expense of any positive contribution it might conceivably have made. The spirit of the constitution has in turn permeated the system of law that has ramified from it, with the consequence that state law, and particularly the part of the law that rests upon judicial decisions, is more concerned with what the state cannot do than with what it can do. It would be strange indeed if this spirit of negativism had not made its presence felt in the legislative and administrative branches of the state's government. The temper of the government of the typical state, from constitution to courts to operating divisions, is unmistakably negative. The official spends more time looking over his shoulder than he does scanning the horizon.

Fourth, in part as a natural consequence of the foregoing, in part because their makers consciously wanted it that way, the state constitutions contain a great deal of what most knowledgeable observers regard as excessive detail. Whatever its virtues otherwise, a document that runs to almost a thousand pages (as does the constitution of Louisiana) can hardly be said to be a constitution in any proper sense. Louisiana's constitution is the classic example, but many others suffer from the disease of overexplicitness in greater or less degree. California's constitution, as an example, runs to 75,000 words, including (after sixty years of experience) 343 amendments. One might suppose that New York would have a reasonably adequate basic charter; not so, according to an official commission, which concluded, "The constitution of the State of New York is not a constitution in a proper constitutional sense. It is a mass of legal texts, some truly fundamental and appropriate to a constitution, others a maze of statutory detail, and many obsolete or meaningless in present times."[6] Our three examples include the two most populous states in the Union, both of them generally thought to be well-governed. It appears that both leave much to be desired in the matter of the fundamental charter under which the state is governed.

The excessive attention to detail that characterizes the typical constitution has two untoward results for modern government. First is the loss in flexibility which flows from the effort to foresee and cover every contingency. Second, and closely related, is the straitjacket in which the torrent of constitutional verbiage constricts the government. A particular victim of the constitution's specificity is the muncipality, whose government frequently is described in great detail. In a larger sense, of course, the state as a whole is the loser through the efforts of the drafters of the constitution to achieve

---

[6] The Temporary Commission on the Revision and Simplification of the Constitution, *First Steps Toward a Modern Constitution*, State of New York, Legislative Document No. 58 (1959), p. 1.

complete coverage of every significant subject. In a word, the state is shackled by its constitution; far from being released to perform important tasks with reasonable discretion, the government is rendered virtually immobile by the very document to which it looks for motive force.

If the state at large is the loser through these constitutional inadequacies, the cities are particular victims. The cities do not require a favored place in the constitution, but they do require a state government that is cognizant of current (and prospective) trends, is able and willing to take positive action, and is in forward motion. These qualities unhappily do not characterize the typical state government, which appears content to maintain the *status quo.* This spirit of complacency is of course not traceable solely to constitutional deficiencies, though these must bear a good part of the responsibility.

The New York commission cited above listed three requisites for a satisfactory constitutional article on local government:

1. It should promote local self-government by providing for a broad, unambiguous grant of power to local governments that will stimulate initiative and vigor in meeting new and expanding responsibilities.

2. It should permit maximum intergovernmental cooperation in meeting problems that cannot be handled properly by each local government acting alone.

3. It should free the legislature of the burden of acting on hosts of local bills so that it may concentrate on matters of importance to the whole state.[7]

It is scarcely necessary to affirm that no constitution contains a local government article that meets these specifications with complete satisfaction, and that most fall short by a wide measure. State constitutions do not afford their governments much assistance in dealing with the problems of modern society, let alone those occasioned by the surge of the cities.

REPRESENTATIVE GOVERNMENT

In America democracy and representative government are inseparably linked, and in state government the prime representative

[7] *Ibid.,* p. 15.

institution is the legislature. Notwithstanding the Will Rogers dictum that "It is better to have termites in your house than to have the legislature in session," the legislative body is the chief repository of the hope for good government in the state. If it serves well, the state functions well; if it earns and keeps a reputation for morality, the state enjoys a good reputation. The legislature is in truth the foundation of democratic government.

If the legislature is the state's major representative body, of what is it representative? Each state legislature except that of Nebraska has two bodies—the upper house, called the senate, and the lower house. The concepts of representation applied to the two are by no means identical, nor do the concepts applied in one state necessarily coincide with those embraced in another. Many schemes have been evolved to achieve representativeness according to the lights of their many sponsors. William Boyd has identified seven patterns of apportionment for the lower house and as many as nine for the senate, which either are in effect or are seriously proposed for consideration by one or several of the fifty states.[8] Briefly, these "variations on a theme" may be reduced to three. They are population, political subdivisions (counties, towns), and geographical areas ("country"). The three bases have been otherwise rendered as people, prairies, and pine trees. They are put together in varying combinations from state to state to produce Boyd's more extended list.

State legislative apportionment has been subjected to heavy criticism over many years, and on three main grounds. First, the

---

[8] William J. D. Boyd, *Patterns of Apportionment* (New York: National Municipal League, 1962). There is a considerable and growing literature on legislative apportionment and reapportionment, much of it spurred by the recent interest taken in the subject by the Supreme Court. As in the case of state constitutions, the National Municipal League has exhibited a lively concern in proper legislative apportionment. The League has published a number of studies in the field in recent years, and its monthly publication, the *National Civic Review,* is extremely useful as a handbook, particularly for current developments. *The Politics of Reapportionment,* edited by Malcolm E. Jewell (New York: Atherton Press, 1962), comprises a series of highly informative essays on the subject. A report by the Advisory Commission on Intergovernmental Relations, *Apportionment of State Legislatures* (Washington, D.C.: ACIR, 1962), likewise provides a thoughtful and useful treatment.

bases employed have been questioned sharply. Some critics maintain that the "federal analogy" has no validity when applied to the state legislature, as it is in California. Vermont's system, under which one representative is given to each town regardless of population, places a hamlet of 38 inhabitants on an equal footing with the state's largest city, which in 1960 had a population of 35,531. Others aver that there is more to the representative function than people alone; the representative, they insist, must also bear in mind the values and virtues that inhere in the land, and so must represent area as well as population. Chief among contemporary critics of acreage or place as a basis for representation is the Supreme Court itself, whose position we shall examine presently. Without analyzing in detail the bases for representation, we may conclude that they constitute a central point of criticism of legislative apportionment.

A second criticism turns on the results achieved by prevailing systems. In 1926, for example, California adopted a constitutional amendment which provided that no county should have more than one senator and no senatorial district should include more than three counties. Under this arrangement the most populous county in the state (Los Angeles County with more than 6 million people) has one senator, while a rural district with 14,294 people also has one. The three largest counties in 1960 had about 51 per cent of the state's population, but only three out of forty senators. Less than 11 per cent of the population scattered among rural and mountain areas could control the senate—and this is a state whose metropolitan population comprises more than 86 per cent of the total. The conflict here is of course between northern California and the explosively expanding southern counties. The same conflict prevails in Florida, where twenty-two rural-minded senators (of a total of thirty-eight) have banded together in a "Pork Chop Gang" to protect the values—and the political power—of the small towns and counties. The victim of their resistance is rapidly growing south Florida, where five urban counties with more than 50 per cent of the state's population (1960) have less than 16 per cent of the seats in the lower house and a correspondingly small proportion of the seats in the senate. The country over, 14 per cent or less of the population could control the senate in five states (Nevada, California, Arizona,

New Mexico, and Florida), while 20 per cent or less of the population could control the lower house in five states (Vermont, Connecticut, Delaware, Kansas, and Missouri). It will be observed that these states are widely scattered, and that several of them have experienced rapid urban growth during the last two decades.

A third criticism of state apportionment systems grows from the failure of many states to reapportion on a systematic and periodic basis. Perhaps the most notorious offender in this regard is Alabama, where there was no reapportionment from 1901 to the early 1960s notwithstanding a constitutional requirement of reapportionment every ten years. During these six decades the population of Birmingham had grown from 38,415 to 340,887, and the state's urban population had increased from less than 12 per cent of the total to almost 55 per cent. Alabama has of course not been the sole offender, for other states also have failed to honor their constitutional requirements for periodic reapportionment. Moreover, where reapportionment has come it has frequently been grudging in spirit and minimal in effect. Few states have sought to reapportion in a way to introduce true balance into their legislative bodies.

The apportionment and reapportionment of state legislatures has long been held to be exclusively a state responsibility, and the national government historically has consistently pursued a hands-off policy. In particular, the federal courts have refused to accept jurisdiction over cases involving legislative apportionment. In 1962, however, the Supreme Court changed this time-honored position dramatically by taking judicial cognizance of a Tennessee case involving apportionment. The basis for the Court's assertion of jurisdiction was the "equal protection of the laws" clause of the Fourteenth Amendment, which had until that time been uniformly rejected as a basis for entertaining apportionment cases. The case in question, *Baker v. Carr,* was significant because it threw the federal courts open to cases involving legislative malapportionment.[9] In its decision the Court used such terms as "arbitrary and capricious" and "invidious discrimination" in citing grounds for questioning state action. What the case might mean in practical application could not be foreseen in 1962.

[9] *Baker v. Carr,* 369 U.S. 186 (1962).

Its significance began to emerge in a series of decisions handed down by the Supreme Court on June 15, 1964. The decisions involved legislative apportionment in six states: Alabama, Colorado, Delaware, Maryland, New York, and Virginia.[10] The Court uniformly found the systems of legislative districts unconstitutional, invoking the equal-protection-of-the-laws clause in each instance. Noting, in the Alabama case, that "State Legislatures are, historically, the fountainhead of representative government in this country," the Court proceeded to demolish Alabama's archaic system of legislative districting. Three quotations will serve to indicate the gist of the Court's reasoning:

> How then can one person be given twice or ten times the voting power of another person in a statewide election merely because he lives in a rural area or because he lives in the smallest rural county?

> Legislators represent people, not trees or acres. Legislators are elected by voters, not farms or cities or economic interests.

> A nation once primarily rural in character becomes predominantly urban. Representation schemes once fair and equitable become archaic and outdated. But the basic principle of representative government remains, and must remain, unchanged—the weight of a citizen's vote cannot be made to depend on where he lives. Population is, of necessity, the starting point for consideration and the controlling criterion for judgment in legislative apportionment controversies.[11]

The Supreme Court thus identified population as the true constitutional basis for legislative apportionment. In so doing it embraced without cavil the principle summarized in "one citizen, one vote." It held, moreover, that *both* houses of the legislature are subject to this rule.

The apportionment controversy of the last few years has produced action on three other fronts. First, the states have turned to

[10] Alabama: *Reynolds v. Sims,* 84 S. Ct. 1362 (1964); Colorado: *Lucas v. the Forty-Fourth General Assembly of the State of Colorado,* 84 S. Ct. 1472 (1964); Delaware: *Roman v. Sincock,* 84 S. Ct. 1462 (1964); Maryland: *Maryland Committee for Fair Representation v. Tawes,* 84 S. Ct. 1442 (1964); New York: *WMCA, Inc., v. Lomenzo,* 84 S. Ct. 1418 (1964); Virginia: *Davis v. Mann,* 84 S. Ct. 1453 (1964).

[11] *Reynolds v. Sims,* pp. 1379 (citing *Gray v. Sanders,* 372 U.S. 368, 1963), 1382, and 1384.

the apportionment problem with a zeal quite without precedent. The current activity in the field dated from *Baker v. Carr;* for if the states could not read the handwriting on the wall from that case they could at least divine its message. True, state action for the most part has been taken without enthusiasm, in the spirit suggested by the question, "What is the least we can do to satisfy the Court?" True, further, it has resulted for the most part from legal suits. Still, there has been action, in as many as forty-two states, since the Baker case. There is evidence that the Court will not be satisfied with minimal or nominal modifications in malapportionment practices, though it is entirely likely that many states will move only slowly and haltingly toward the goal fixed by the 1964 decisions.

Second, the states reacted in anger to *Baker v. Carr* by sponsoring a series of three amendments to the Constitution of the United States. The amendments, which were proposed by two legislative branches of the Council of State Governments (the organization of the states), would have modified the union in drastic fashion by reducing it, competent observers have declared, from a federal system to a confederacy. They would have had the effect of removing from federal purview all concern for or control over legislative apportionment, reserving responsibility for action in that field solely to the states. The proposed amendments failed for want of support in Congress. The states then turned to an effort to have Congress call a constitutional convention to propose an amendment allowing states to base apportionment in one house of the legislature on "factors other than population." Congress would be obliged to call such a convention if it should receive identical joint resolutions passed by two-thirds of the state legislatures. By April 1965 fewer than twenty legislatures had passed the resolutions, and competent observers were doubtful that the move would succeed. These activities suggest that the states, or some of them—the number of confirmed dissidents appears to stand at about one-third of the total— will not soon accept the Supreme Court's ruling with grace or enthusiasm.[12]

[12] See *The Dis-Union Proposals,* a reprint comprising three articles published in the *National Civic Review* of September 1963 (New York: National Municipal League, 1963). For the early 1965 developments, see

Third, Congress took notice of the hubbub created by the Court's assertion of jurisdiction over apportionment cases. Expressions there ranged from vigorous approval to outrage, and these diverse views found reflection in a variety of proposals for congressional action. The one that appeared to command widest support called for a stay of application of the Court's redistricting order until 1966. Neither this nor any other protest proposal gained approval in the 1964 session; perhaps the results of the national elections of that year, together with the civil rights developments of 1965, will prove permanently to have chilled congressional ardor for battle on the reapportionment issue.

The significance of legislative apportionment for the cities is great. As we have noted, malapportionment weighs heaviest on the urban centers, while failure to reapportion strikes hardest at the centers of greatest population growth, that is, at the cities. Reapportionment is rightly understood to be primarily a rural-urban issue; it was so identified by the Supreme Court in a passage from the recent Alabama case. Nowhere does rural determination to cling to control manifest itself more nakedly than in connection with state legislative apportionment.

There are those who maintain that the cities would not profit materially from a wholesale reapportionment based on population. These observers point out that some of the largest cities currently are losing population to the suburbs, which therefore would be the effective beneficiaries of any massive reapportionment. There is the further fact, they go on to say, that reapportionment would not benefit the metropolitan areas, because legislative districts are not drawn to conform to metropolitan configurations, and increased representation for the city and the suburbs would not add up to increased metropolitan representation. Others note that there are differences in interest and point of view among cities—between New York City and the urban upstate centers, for example. Others still observe that a rural-*minded* legislator is not always a *rural* legislator, that lawmakers from the cities, sometimes sizable cities, frequently ally themselves with rural representatives in thought and action. The

"Several States Back 'Other Factors' Plan," *National Civic Review*, vol. LIV, no. 3 (March 1965), pp. 151–154.

legislators from New York's upstate cities, to cite a familiar example, are fundamentally rural in outlook and association. The net result is the view that the rural-urban dichotomy is a false one, and that in any event the alleged community of interest among the cities is far from monolithic.

To argue thus is in a sense to beg the question. The logic seems to lead to the conclusion that the cities have no general stake in the composition of the state legislature, which of course cannot be allowed. Reduced to simplest terms, the interests of the cities are the interests of the state, because the cities in many instances *are* the state, and because cities and state will tend increasingly to draw together in their basic concerns. Beyond that, the cities undeniably would profit from even gradual or partial substitution at the state house of an urban point of view for the presently prevailing rural orientation. What is required is not a legislative body that will attend exclusively to the affairs of the city, but rather one that will address the problems of modern society. Urban America will improve in prospect if the state legislatures can be reconstituted in a way that will cause them to reflect the temper and the aspirations of a post-midcentury nation.

Still, let us not dismiss too lightly the thought that massive reapportionment could have immediate and direct consequences for the urban centers. Consider the case of Georgia, where abolition of the notorious unit rule resulted in the nomination and election in 1962 of an urban candidate for governor for the first time in this century. Who can say with assurance that similar miracles may not occur elsewhere?

ORGANIZATION FOR ADMINISTRATION

Two circumstances attendant upon the American Revolution determined the course of the executive branch of government for well over a hundred years. First was the general experience with executive officers during colonial days. The King himself commanded little affection or respect, and the typical governor did nothing to improve the image of the executive. To the colonists, the governor symbolized their troubles with the Crown, and for want of access to the sovereign they fastened on him the responsibility for their mounting difficulties. Thus, at the time the state governments were established, the governor and all associated with him almost universally were held in low repute. Second was the wide commitment to the principles of democracy as the term was understood in that day. Excepting in the local communities the colonists had had little experience of democracy under British rule. In a general sense, however, they understood the word to stand for responsible government. The problem of making the legislative body popularly responsible appeared not insurmountable; that of devising a responsible executive branch, however, seemed considerably more complex. A prime preoccupation of the early constitution drafters was to establish an executive office that would be democratically responsible.

The problem was approached through application of the principle of separation of powers, an arrangement which ensured that the governor would enjoy only certain specified powers, and that he would have to take into account both the legislative and the judicial branches in their exercise. The separation of powers, together with the corollary doctrine of checks and balances, is rightly regarded as one of America's principal contributions to the art of governance. It remains a major conditioner of the office of governor to this day.

Another approach to the problem of executive responsibility witnessed the installation of popular controls over the executive branch. The governor, and presently many other administrative officials, were made subject to election by popular vote. Their terms were short: two years came to be standard; and there was a limitation on the number of terms an official (more specifically, the governor) might serve: a single re-election came to be the rule. In the fullness of time the recall was added to the democratic arsenal, so that a governor or other high administrative official might be removed from office by popular action before the end of his term.

Even with these popular safeguards a lurking fear remained of a tyrannical executive. Another major control device would prevent the rise of an autocratic governor by dividing the executive power among many officials, each of whom in turn would be subjected to popular controls. This reasoning led to the proliferation of the normal executive departments and later to the wide use of boards and commissions for executive and quasi-executive functions. The time would come when executive responsibilities would be divided among a hundred or more departments and agencies in a given state. No matter; if executive power was fragmented beyond effective use, it was by that very fact placed beyond usurpation by a would-be tyrant.

Finally, the application of democratic principles to the executive branch called for an amateur civil service. President Jackson popularized the philosophy behind this concept, but in so doing he had ample precedent. There is no doubt that the notion of public service rendered by lay citizens was squarely in the democratic tradition.

Two features of the environment of executive development are worthy of special mention. First, the emphasis was almost wholly on the perfection and maintenance of democratic controls, to the substantial exclusion of considerations of administrative effectiveness. The latter was not even recognized as a desirable quality of state government in the early days; for vigorous administration smacked of a strong executive and so was anathema to those who planned the new governments. Second, and as a consequence of the foregoing, the emphasis was preponderantly on limitations on the executive branch; almost never was there a positive statement concerning the powers of the governor. Thus were native fear and distrust of the King's governor translated into unrelieved negativism respecting the executive branch of the new governments.

The crude application of the principles outlined produced unhappy and unanticipated consequences for the executive branch of the state's government. In such an unfriendly atmosphere none but a weak and flaccid governor could exist. It would not have been proper to speak of the state's chief executive during the nineteenth century, for there was no chief executive. There was at best a *primus inter pares,* with a number of executive officers operating in substantial independence of the nominal head. Nor was there effective leadership, for the ingredients of vigorous executive action were almost wholly lacking.

In terms of organization, the state's administration was a rambling, unplanned structure wherein a wide variety of agencies operated in substantial independence each of all the rest. As late as

1950, well into the reorganization period, Alabama had 117 state agencies, Ohio 122, Texas 124; many enjoyed constitutional status—the constitution of Oklahoma recognized 33 offices and agencies, that of New York 27, that of Michigan 19. Most administrative agencies possessed considerable independence; those with constitutional protection operated in an isolation that was splendid indeed. In essence the typical state had not one government but ten or twenty. To speak of coordinating the state's manifold administrative agencies was to indulge in daydreams, more particularly because the nominal head of the state could scarcely be identified among the army of officials.

In another direction, financial procedures were inadequate and ill-conceived. Typically there was no state budget, only a series of individual departmental and agency budgets, and such budgetary responsibility as could be identified ran to the legislature rather than to the governor's office. Accounting practices were haphazard, and the purchase of supplies was left to the separate agencies. There was nothing approaching an adequate audit. In short, no one office was charged with responsibility for financial management.

Finally, the amateur civil service given philosophical justification by President Jackson degenerated into the spoils system, a phenomenon so widely known even now as to require no description. There was a rude rationale for the spoils system in terms of democratic theory, but the feeling that its evils outweighed its goods came to prevail almost universally.

In the evolution of a system of administration which most observers regarded as a perversion of democratic intention, two other institutions played highly significant roles. On the one hand, many agencies enjoyed constitutional status, and so were beyond reach by normal action. Moreover, many questionable practices were embalmed in the constitution, which was filled with a mass of statutory detail. On the other hand, the legislature found itself unable to take action to improve administration even when permitted by the constitution to do so, for it was itself a party to the process which reduced administration to the level described. Thus did the constitution and the legislature contribute to the state's administrative deficiencies.

The situation summarized persisted throughout the nineteenth century, and indeed well into the twentieth. Two trends, however, were taking form which were to call existing administrative practice sharply into question. For all the blows sustained by the governor throughout the last century, that officer nevertheless showed increasing signs of emerging as the focal point of the state's administration. His fight was uphill all the way and he suffered many reverses along the road; nevertheless by the end of the century he had taken on the appearance of *the* chief executive in many states. His major weapon lay in the simple but potent fact that, when circumstances required leadership, there was no place to look but to the office of governor. In a century-long war in which the legislature was his principal adversary, the governor forged to the front as head of the state. By the end of the century it was clear that the office of governor offered the only practical repository for the executive powers of the state.

The second trend witnessed the rise of administration as an aspect of government worthy of special notice. Woodrow Wilson, writing in the mid-eighties, was among the first to speak of administration as a subject of inherent importance. Administration, he said, concerns the way the government transacts its affairs; it has to do with the employment and deployment of men, with civil servants and their organization for the execution of public programs. The concept of administration *as administration,* and of its critical role in the process of government, is familiar to the America of 1965, but it was so novel as to be revolutionary eight decades ago. Wilson's views rapidly gained wide acceptance, fortified as they were on the action side by Frederick W. Taylor; and in the course of time a new approach to human activity was born. In industry it was called scientific management, in government simply public administration. In both it emphasized the organization and ordering of the energies of men in the achievement of designated tasks or programs. The distinction between politics and administration need not detain us; it is enough that politics commanded almost exclusive attention until about 1885, whereas after that time it was forced more and more to share the public stage with administration. The governor had already established himself as the state's political leader; he was soon to emerge as its administrative head as well.

It was inevitable that the mounting concern for administration should eventuate in criticism of existing organization and practice and in proposals for reform. Public discussion and private study of the subject found practical expression in the movement for administrative reorganization which, interestingly enough, swept federal, state, and local governments almost simultaneously. President Taft took the first definite step by appointing a Commission on Economy and Efficiency in the national government in 1910. The city manager plan, which came into being at about the same time, was the most dramatic manifestation of the reorganization movement in local government. State commissions on administrative reorganization were appointed: one in Wisconsin in 1911, others in Massachusetts and New Jersey the next year. Enthusiasm for reorganization ran high; here at last was a way to improve the economy and efficiency of government, to get better service for less money from public servants.

State interest in administrative reorganization has been great since the inception of the movement, though two waves of heightened concern may be identified. The first, which was touched off by a general reorganization in Illinois in 1917, was concentrated in the years immediately following World War I. By 1940 about thirty states had undergone reorganizations of varying scope and intensity. The second, which was set in motion by the first Hoover Commission and was soon characterized by numerous state "Little Hoover Commissions," came just following World War II. It witnessed the appointment of reorganization commissions in some thirty-two states. There is, then, and for many years there has been a lively interest in state administrative reorganization.[13]

[13] The literature dealing with state administrative reorganization is extensive. The standard reference for the first phase of the movement is A. E. Buck, *The Reorganization of State Governments in the United States* (New York: National Municipal League, 1938). For the second phase, useful references include *Reorganizing State Government* (Chicago: The Council of State Governments, 1950); York Willbern, "Administration in State Governments," in *The Forty-Eight States* (New York: The American Assembly,

The principles governing state administrative reorganization may be summarized in a few general propositions:

1. The governor is the administrative (as well as the political) head of the state. The office of governor therefore should be exalted rather than minimized.

2. If the governor is to serve effectively as the state's administrative head, he must be given staff aids to enable him to perform his managerial duties effectively. Chief among these are a fiscal staff (notably a budget office) and a planning staff. (This concept is comparable with that of the Executive Office of the President, though in miniature.)

3. The executive departments should be greatly reduced in number (preferably to not more than twelve or fifteen), and should be organized along functional lines. "Short ballot" principles should prevail; that is, department heads should be appointed rather than elected. Further to emphasize the importance of the office of governor and to give its occupant effective power to direct and coordinate executive activities, the governor should be given the authority to appoint department heads.

4. Independent and quasi-independent agencies (boards and commissions) should be reduced to the minimum number deemed absolutely necessary. The most desirable number is zero.

5. The system of fiscal management should be drastically overhauled. The minimum essential reforms included an executive budget, an effective accounting system, and a central purchasing office, all statewide in coverage. The responsibilities of fiscal management can best be discharged through an integrated department of finance or department of administration. The new department should be closely associated with the office of governor, and its head should be his right-hand man.

1955); and two studies published by the National Municipal League in connection with its State Constitutional Studies Project: Bennett M. Rich, *State Constitutions: The Governor* (1960), and Ferrell Heady, *State Constitutions: The Structure of Administration* (1961). *The Book of the States,* published biennially by The Council of State Governments, provides a useful summary of contemporary developments.

6. The fiscal records of the state should be subject to an independent audit, performed by an auditor either elected by the people or chosen by the legislature.

7. The state should adopt a strong merit system and give it the widest possible coverage. (The merit system movement and the administrative reorganization movement had separate origins, but have gone along hand-in-hand nevertheless. A strong merit system is deemed an essential component of good administration, therefore those who advocate administrative reorganization either support the merit system as part of their program or take such a system for granted.)

On balance, what has been the impact of the administrative reorganization movement on state government? Some observers maintain that specialists in administration err in their efforts to separate administration and politics because, they aver, these are but opposite sides of a coin labeled "government." The drive, they say, should be for the improvement of government in its totality, not of administration alone. Others point to the illogic they discover in the effort to combine administrative and political leadership in the same person. The governor was elected to office as a politician, and he will succeed or fail in office in accordance with his skill as a politician. He must be a political leader first, an administrator only incidentally. Still others note that a large proportion of all recommendations for reorganization fail to win the approval necessary to their effectuation. In particular, legislatures are prone either to scoff at or to ignore proposals for administrative reorganization. Others yet argue that reorganization plans, where adopted, frequently result in little real change. The employees affected continue to perform their duties about as they did before, with neither more nor less energy, skill, or devotion to the public welfare.

In assessing these criticisms it will prove useful to note that there are two kinds of administrative reorganization. The first may be called revolutionary, in that it happens all at once and with dramatic effect. This is what most observers mean when they speak of reorganization. When critics say that such reorganization has not achieved all that has been claimed for it, their charge has more than a kernel of validity. The second variety may be termed evolutionary; it goes on all the time throughout government as administrators seek ways of strengthening their organizations and procedures to the end that services may be improved. Looked at in this light, administrative reorganization has achieved much through incremental improvements during the last half-century—more, there is good reason to suspect, than has been achieved through the frontal assault of revolution. There has in fact been considerable progress toward the attainment of reorganization goals. The office of governor has been strengthened by equipping it with staff aids; a number of departments of administration have been established, usually in close liaison with the governor's office; financial practices have been improved through adoption of the executive budget, sound accounting practice, central procurement and property management, and better auditing procedures; and merit principles have been widely installed for the management of personnel (in 1963, thirty states had broad-coverage merit systems). Critics may assert that these are not legitimate goals, but they can hardly deny the claim that there has been considerable progress of recent years toward their fulfillment.

What is important is the present condition of state administration. Is it static or mobile, effective or ineffective in carrying on public programs, improving or deteriorating? The answer to this general payoff question must be equivocal, for it must rest upon a value judgment. The judgment seems warranted that administrative arrangements are perhaps equal to reasonable and normal demands. The state stands most in want not of improved administration—though that remains an ever present need—but of constitutional reform, legislative reapportionment, and leadership. The last is everywhere in short supply, for whatever the reorganization movement has achieved it has not produced leaders adequate either in number or in vision. This was neither its primary goal nor its promise, but a well-organized administrative structure without vigorous direction falls short of achieving good administration. The state is better equipped in point of organization than in point of leadership.

RESOURCES

The resources commanded by the state are several. First is the reservoir of legal power at its disposal, which is both wide and deep. Second is the state's government, which, in addition to being the only public organization with statewide jurisdiction, possesses several kinds of special strengths. One of these, to illustrate, is the varied array of technicians in its employ, which equips it to provide technical assistance of many kinds to its local governments. Third is leadership: only the governor (along with his administrative associates) is in a position to acquire a broad and firm grasp of state problems and to propose a rational course of action regarding them. Whether the leadership potential is realized in practice is another question. Fourth is money, for the state has access to the wide and varied sources of public funds which make government possible. If its fiscal resources are exploited with courage and funds allocated with judgment, the service needs of the state and its people will be met. The other resources have meaning in good part as they relate to the acquisition, management, and distribution of public funds. The discussion here will center on the state's financial resources.[14]

There was a time not long since when state revenue systems were simple and relatively undifferentiated. Chief reliance was placed in the general property tax, and state programs expanded or contracted as property owners were able (and willing) to support them. Currently, however, reliance is placed on other sources. Chief among these is the sales tax, which in 1962 produced 38.6 per cent of all state general revenue. The second most prolific source was federal grants and subsidies, which contributed 22.8 per cent of the

[14] The following discussion depends for data on two reports by the U.S. Bureau of the Census, *Historical Summary of Governmental Finances in the United States,* 1957, and *Summary of Governmental Finances in 1960, 1961, and 1962.* For assistance with interpretation it leans on Jesse Burkhead, *State and Local Taxes for Public Education* (Syracuse, N.Y.: Syracuse University Press, 1963), and Alan K. Campbell, "State and Local Revenue: A Continuing Crisis" (a processed paper presented at the National Municipal League's National Conference on Government, Detroit, Michigan, November 19, 1963).

total. In third place was the income tax, individual and corporate, which produced 13 per cent. A fourth major contributor was lumped together under the heading of "Charges"; it produced 10 per cent of the total. These four principal sources, then, contributed 84.4 per cent of the total general revenue; together they form the backbone of a state's revenue system.

Campbell points out that this system congealed in its present form some years ago.[15] Thus one must go back twenty years or more to find any marked variation from the pattern summarized. An analysis of recent trends indicates that, *as a percentage contribution to the total revenue,* the income tax increased its contribution 29 per cent from 1952 to 1962, charges increased 25 per cent, and federal subsidies 31.4 per cent. Sales taxes, on the contrary, diminished in their contribution from 1952 to 1962; the 1962 yield, as a percentage of the state general revenue, was considerably less than it had been in 1940. Nevertheless, the sales tax remained the largest single contributor in 1962, and by a considerable margin.

The trends in the states' general revenue pattern over the last quarter-century may be summarized to advantage in a few words. First, the states have gradually moved toward abandonment of the general property tax, leaving that revenue source to the local governments. Second, increasing reliance has been placed on two major dragnet taxes of relatively recent origin. Thirty-seven states now have sales taxes while thirty-four have an individual income tax. All but two states have one or the other. As a collateral trend, the states have moved toward adoption of income tax withholding laws as a means of improving collections; twenty-eight states now have such laws.[16]

Perhaps the most significant trend of all is that which concerns the federal contribution to the general revenue of the states. In 1940 the national government's component was 15.2 per cent of the total; by 1962 it had grown to 22.8 per cent. The increase in its proportion of the general revenue in slightly more than twenty years there-

---

[15] Alan K. Campbell, *op. cit.,* pp. 12–13.

[16] *The Book of the States* is a useful reference for current developments, in finance as in other areas. A standing section on "Finance" (for the last several volumes it has been Section V) affords both statistics and commentary which make possible generalizations on trends.

fore was 50 per cent. There is of course no assurance that this growth trend will continue, but even now the national contribution to state revenue is a vital one. If the state is to meet the support requirements of its expanding public services, particularly the newer ones, with even reasonable success, the contributions of the national government must be continued at a high level. It is quite likely that they will continue and even increase, and most unlikely that they will substantially decline.

In point of simple physical fact the states have the same access to taxable values as the national government, for the sum total of all property and all income in the United States obviously resides in the states. In their never-ending search for added revenues the states nevertheless confront a variety of special problems. Several such problems seem to be inherent, in that they are inseparable from tradition and from prevailing circumstances. Illustrative of these is the fact that a state tax is by nature close to home; the legislator represents a small and frequently intimate district, and his constituents can and do rebuke him personally for any new or increased tax. Again, some potential sources of revenue are beyond the grasp of the state, and are more suited to exploitation by a larger government. Yet again, the consequences of an unbalanced budget become immediately apparent at the state level, for the gap between revenue and expenditure must be closed if the state is to preserve its financial rating. Similarly, arrangements must be made to pay a state debt at the time it is created, and the schedule of payments must be adhered to. Not so the federal government, whose resources (symbolized by the Federal Reserve System) are such as to permit it to run deficits and incur new indebtedness with relative impunity.[17]

Another kind of problem inheres in the political process. It finds permanent manifestation in the competition for resources, competition by interested parties and organizations for support for a variety of service programs as wide as the spectrum of state activities. The allocation of resources in response to these competitive demands is of the essence of both politics and democracy, and few would have it different; but the process does not necessarily result in the opti-

[17] Jesse Burkhead has discussed these and other institutional factors in a very useful way. *Op. cit.*, pp. 8–17.

mum utilization of scarce resources. One concomitant, or consequence, of the allocation process is reflected in the earmarked revenues and special funds which occur in such abundance. An example is the earmarking of gasoline tax revenues for highway construction—an obeisance toward the automobile and all who derive pleasure and profit from it. To the extent that the state's revenues are prededicated to special purposes or uses, the decision-makers (governor together with legislature) are limited in the course they may pursue; they are prisoners of the society at whose hands they exercise the power (but only a limited power) of decision. Yet another aspect of the problem is seen in the limitations on both tax rate and indebtedness which are found in many state constitutions. These go back in their origin to the political process; more to the point, they reflect public distrust in the judgment or integrity of those charged with responsibility for the state's financial affairs.

The process of resource allocation thus is plagued by a disturbing contradiction. On the one hand, the distribution of revenues among services and programs would profit from the widest possible flexibility. In logic, at least, the governor and the legislature are in a position to evaluate both contemporary needs and the factors that should be taken to account in meeting them. But on the other hand, the options available to the decision-makers are severely circumscribed by earmarked revenues, special funds, and constitutional tax and debt limitations. A governor and a legislative body with control over no more than half of the state's annual expenditure cannot properly be held responsible for deciding how and for what purposes the state's money shall be spent. As illustration, discretion over spending for highways was long since eliminated through embrace of a long-range policy commitment to which none can see an end.

The final problem to be noted here arises from the lively competition among the states for industry. This occasions a bifurcated and quite illogical policy whereby the state makes tax concessions designed to keep the industries it has and kindred but not identical concessions to encourage the establishment or immigration of new industry. Jesse Burkhead observes that tax policy is not always or necessarily a determining factor in industrial location, but he also notes that by public consensus the situation is otherwise.[18] There are few influences on the state revenue structure to equal the threat of reprisal by industry.

In summary, state revenue systems confront many and varied problems, some political, some economic, some institutional. Some are inherent in the American system of government and so must be lived with—but not necessarily in their most virulent form; others, however, are remediable. Among the latter is the inflexibility that characterizes the revenue system. The elimination or amelioration of the limitations would not lead automatically to a more rational system of revenue or revenue allocation, but it would constitute a long first step in that direction.

In broad terms, state revenue systems must serve two kinds of needs. First are the continuing requirements for the support of ongoing programs. For these the expenditure pattern is well established. Schools, highways, welfare activities, health and hospitals—each program clientele knows what it is supposed to get and what by long custom it will get as a fraction of the total sum available. It is extremely difficult for new services and programs to break into the closed society represented by the old-timers. Yet these new programs represent, so to speak, the cutting edge of society. Conviction, commitment, and custom all decree that we shall have roads and schools; but shall we have also an urban environment congenial to human fulfillment? Can the state's revenue pattern be altered in a way that will enable it to meet the needs of an urban society?

There is little to suggest that the states recognize any need to accommodate their revenue systems to changing requirements. No substantial new revenue source has been opened up in years, though established sources have gained markedly in productivity. No knowl-

[18] *Ibid.,* pp. 41–42. In this domain among many others rumor normally is more than a match for reason. Individual industries are well aware of the implications, political and otherwise, when they cite a "favorable tax climate" as the reason for continuing in (or coming into) a state and an "unfavorable" climate as the reason for moving out. The reasons for a move may be manifold—changing technology, new products, new markets, plant obsolescence, and so on; but the single reason almost invariably cited is an "unfriendly" tax structure.

edgeable observers anticipate any drastic new development; on the contrary, all expect that the trends which have characterized the last decade will carry forward through the next. *The Book of the States* is instructive in this connection. Noting that "more than half of the states found it necessary to expand their tax systems in 1962 or 1963 [to meet] pressures for added spending. . . ," it observed that "enactments were directed principally at increasing the productivity of existing systems, rather than at an overhaul of the systems."[19] The policy of "constant improvement but no yearly models" may lead to the minimal alleviation of some of the problems just discussed, but it is not likely to strengthen the state revenue system appreciably. The prospect is not bright that the states will rise to the challenge of an urban society through adequate monetary support of necessary new or expanded services. In this context the contribution made by the national government to state general revenue looms larger than ever. The opinion may be hazarded that the part played by the federal government will become increasingly important as the years pass.

PROGRAMS

In 1962 the expenditures of the states totaled $36.4 billion. Education accounted for 34.3 per cent of all general expenditures, highways for 25.5 per cent, public welfare for 13.7 per cent, and health and hospitals for 7.5 per cent. The remaining 19 per cent was divided among a number of purposes, including natural resources, correction, police, employment security administration, financial administration, general control, and miscellaneous and unallocable.[20]

Included in the total expenditure figure was an item labeled "intergovernmental expenditure," otherwise sometimes listed as "state payments to local governments" and known popularly as "state aid." This category of expenditure concerns us here; although state expenditures in substantive areas (education, highways, and so on) obviously affect the cities, state aid reflects an immediate and a direct concern for local government. We can look here for an

[19] *The Book of the States, 1964–1965,* p. 226.
[20] *Ibid.,* pp. 200–201.

expression of state monetary interest in urban affairs as such.

State intergovernmental expenditure in 1962 totaled $10.9 billion. Although state aid has increased rapidly in absolute terms over the years—from 1942 to 1962 the dollar growth was sixfold— it has declined gradually as a proportion of total state general expenditure. As long ago as 1942 the proportion was 39.1 per cent, in 1952 it was 36.8 per cent, in 1962, 34.9 per cent. In 1942, state intergovernmental expenditure amounted to 25 per cent of total local government revenue; for 1952, the comparable figure was 29.8 per cent, and for 1962, 28.2 per cent.[21] State aid to local governments is, therefore, a long-established and well-understood practice. The states expect to dedicate somewhat more than one-third of each year's general expenditure to the aid of local governments, which in turn count on state payments for over one-fourth of their total revenue.

It is not with gross figures that we are chiefly concerned here, but with the distribution of the payments made. In 1962, almost half (49.5 per cent) of the $10.9 billion total went to school districts; counties ranked second among recipients with 28 per cent, and municipalities third with 18.7 per cent. Functionally the sum was distributed thus: general local government support, 7.7 per cent; education, 59.4 per cent; public welfare, 16.3 per cent; highways, 12.2 per cent; hospitals and health, 1.7 per cent; and miscellaneous and combined, 2.7 per cent. These figures do not represent *state* expenditures in these functional fields, but rather state aid in support of the local activities designated.

The major local programs aided by state funds are, like the practice of state aid itself, of long standing and general acceptance; they are, moreover, of basic importance, for few would question their contribution to the well-being of the community. It is well to remember, at the same time, that they are not pointed toward the new and emergent problems of our urban society; except for relatively minor internal adjustments, each program goes along about as it has for the last quarter-century.

[21] U.S. Bureau of the Census, *Census of Governments: 1962,* vol. VI, no. 2, *State Payments to Local Governments,* pp. 1, 9. Heavy reliance is placed on this volume for the data of this section.

We must look, therefore, to the "miscellaneous and combined" category for any expression of special interest the state may have taken in the newer problems of urban America. Under that heading, buried in the individual state reports, are listed such expenditure purposes as civil defense, disaster relief (sometimes flood or tornado relief), policemen and firemen pensions, police salaries, libraries, public housing, urban renewal and redevelopment, airport construction, urban planning, juvenile delinquency—the list is long and varied, but these items appear most frequently. For state payments in support of these activities the cities in 1962 received $172,751,000, which amounted to somewhat less than 1.6 per cent of all state payments to local governments.[22]

The summary figures, however, conceal as well as disclose. Three states (Idaho, Iowa, and West Virginia) made no contributions to their cities under the "miscellaneous and combined" category in 1962. It might be proposed in explanation that these are not among the great urban states, but this would not seem persuasive to the six metropolitan areas of Iowa and the four of West Virginia. Also, the individual reports for several states list as "state payments to local governments" federal funds received by the states and passed along to their cities. These are not state payments in any true sense, but rather state transmittals as agents. There is no ready way to learn what these mis-listings amount to in total, though from occasional revealing entries it is evident that they reduce the nominal total by some millions of dollars. Three states—California, New York, and Pennsylvania—in 1962 made 72 per cent of all state payments to local governments. This meant that forty-seven states combined contributed less than $49 million toward the support of the kinds of local activities noted above. The total per capita payment (using 1960 population figures as a basis for the computation) amounted to 96 cents; omitting California, New York, and Pennsylvania, the per capita payment for the remaining forty-seven states was 35.7 cents.

The individual state reports provide further useful information when examined with reference to the urgent urban problems identified in Chapter 1 and the public programs that have been devised

[22] Percentage figures calculated from data presented in *ibid.,* p. 14.

to deal with them. Twelve states reported that in 1962 they made contributions to their cities to aid in airport construction or maintenance. As many as ten reported state payments to cities in support of public housing (often a specified type of housing, as for veterans or the elderly), urban renewal and development, juvenile delinquency programs, pollution abatement, and planning. There was (in 1962 again) no whisper of state support for an urban mass transit program. There have been some accommodations to current and emergent stresses in established city programs enjoying state support, but they have been minimal.

The single overwhelming conclusion to be drawn from this analysis is that the states' concern for the vast new problems of metropolitan America, as measured by monetary contributions toward their alleviation, is quite casual. There is little evidence, indeed, that the states recognize these problems as anything more than very limited state responsibilities. The national government, observing the inability of the cities to meet the new challenges of urbanism alone and the unwillingness of the states to lend them effective assistance, has devised a series of new programs designed to bring the nation's resources to bear on the areas of major stress. These programs generally do not possess the vigor nor do they command the support necessary to deal most effectively with the problems they address, but they do signify a growing awareness by the federal government of the existence of strains beyond the resources of traditional city governments. Unhappily the states do not share that awareness, or share it in only limited degree. Most states have been persuaded to pass the enabling acts necessary to city participation in the federally-aided programs, and several require federal funds destined for the cities to be channeled though state agencies. Such measures, however, reflect nothing more than formal and sometimes grudging action; they do not demonstrate anxiety about or even lively interest in the substantive issues involved. Conclusive evidence of the negative attitude that prevails is found in the data examined above, which indicate that a vast majority of the states have made only minuscule contributions to the programs designed to alleviate the urgent new problems of urban America.

Within the last five years a few states have taken notice of the onrush of urbanism through nonmonetary action. New York established an Office of Local Government, together with a Joint Legislative Committee on Metropolitan Problems. *The Book of the States* reports optimistically on these and like developments, and quotes a resolution adopted by the 1962 Governors' Conference which admonished the states to "move promptly to assert vigorous leadership and to provide effective assistance with respect to problems of governmental structure, finance and planning in metropolitan areas."[23] This is brave sentiment, but the few instances where moves have been made to implement it serve only to emphasize the gap between expression and action. Some states may indeed be edging toward a more energetic urban policy, but there is little evidence to this point of tangible action calculated to effectuate policy. Only vigorous action by all members of the federal family will prove equal to the challenge of the new urban age. To date the states have been unwilling to commit substantial resources to the common effort to meet that challenge.

HORIZONS

Throughout this discussion has run an undertone that needs now to be brought to the surface and made explicit. It concerns the frame of mind which state leaders bring to their tasks, the myths and traditions about government which flow from this attitudinal background, and their consequences for public action.

The frame of thinking of state partisans is characterized by a number of preconceptions that produce a characteristic state mindset. First, the state man is oriented toward the land, his America is a rural society, his values are those of an agrarian way of life. In the enduring lexicon of preindustrial days, honesty, hard work, thrift, and native ingenuity are sufficient to overcome all obstacles. Second, state-oriented thinking occurs within the limits of a rigid moral code which all must publicly profess. It calls for unvarying adherence to revealed and universally embraced public virtues, and its devotees— and these include all who presume to speak for the people—must

[23] *The Book of the States, 1964–1965,* p. 301.

assume a mantle of righteousness. Swift and sure destruction comes to those who deviate. The collapse of the Rockefeller campaign for the 1964 Republican nomination for President is generally attributed to his departure from the personal moral code prescribed for public figures.

Third, the state mind is provincial. It is comfortable in the midst of commonplace things in familiar surroundings. It measures large issues in terms of felt local (that is, personal) experience. It sees state and even national problems as extensions of the petty difficulties of the immediate community. Fourth, at the state level the individualism of the frontier continues to hold sway. Emphasis on personal virtues is accompanied by stress on individual strengths and responsibilities. The single citizen may yet achieve grand goals through his own efforts; any individual who fails to achieve (food and clothing for his family, the "good things" of life, security in old age) obviously is lacking in the basic virtues.

Rural orientation, provincial outlook, commitment to a strict moral code, a philosophy of individualism—these are the components of the state mind. If they evoke memories of the oil lamp and the covered bridge, why this very spirit of nostalgia is also characteristic of the state mind. One of the most unhappy features of the state (and its leaders and institutions) is its intermittent and imperfect contact with the realities of the modern word.[24]

The state of mind just described has given birth to certain myths and traditions which condition state reaction to public policy issues. Chief among these is the conviction that little government— little government in the sense of small local governments, little government in the sense of a minimum of state government—is both virtuous and democratic. Conversely, big government—the big city, the big state, the federal government—is likely to be corrupt and is certain to be undemocratic. Government by friends and neighbors is to be trusted, distant government by bureaucrats (that is, strangers) is not. A corollary praises the virtues of free enterprise, for the corporation is the direct descendant of frontier individualism.

[24] To speak as though all states and all state leaders fit this characterization is, of course, grossly to overgeneralize. Enough do, however, to make the generalization valid, allowing the inevitable exceptions.

Urban problems, the mythology continues, spring from the unhealthy soil, even from the misdeeds, of the city. If the city is the unnatural and unwanted issue of American growth, the difficulties that beset it lack the legitimacy of old-line claimants to public attention. Metropolitan problems are of the same genre; they are not matters with which the state need concern itself.

Aside from considerations of what is right and just, the mythology goes on to assert that the state lacks power to deal with the panoply of problems to which modern society gives rise. Besides, it is not the business of the state to take action every time a "problem" the size of a man's hand blows across the sky. To the assertion of lack of power is added the claim of inadequate resources: in crude terms, the state simply does not have and cannot find the money to support all the public services this, that, and the other segment of society desire.

Finally, the native distrust of big government comes to focus in a particular fear of the federal government, which is frequently seen as an octopus enveloping in its ambitious tentacles larger and larger segments of individual freedom and more and more of state prerogatives. This, indeed, is as nearly universal a state myth as may be found. It accounts for the recurrent efforts to "cut the federal government down to size" by redefining federal-state relations so as to permit the states to exercise their "rightful powers."

This state of mind and the myths growing from it have important consequences for state action. They result in a hard-bitten and almost uniform conservatism: What has been done over a period of years can continue to be done, but what is new and different must be regarded with suspicion. "Legislatures must of necessity be cautious . . . ," they "must of necessity be traditionalists . . . ," a recent state publication proclaimed.[25] The background for state action results in a defensiveness which eyes the federal government with distrust and the cities with dislike. The states are entrenched in the constitution, and what is more to the point those who govern them are strongly ensconced in their seats of

[25] New York, "Senate Administration: First Annual Report of the Secretary of the Senate, 1963" (no place of publication or date, processed), Introduction.

power. They understand well the organizational and procedural ways of state government, and they mean to risk neither position nor power through entertainment of "radical" (that is, new or different) propositions. The spirit of defensiveness and possessiveness resulted long ago in the doctrine of states' rights, which has come to embody the philosophical justification for state intransigence. This then eventuates in a policy and practice of dedicated negativism. Reaction among the states to the Supreme Court decisions of 1964 on legislative reapportionment was almost universally negative. There was a great busyness to learn what the decisions would mean for individual legislators and particular localities and regions, but little note of the promise that they would produce a more representative legislature. Addiction to the *status quo* leads almost invariably to an unfavorable reaction to anything new or strange. Emergent developments are regarded not as harbingers of progress but as threats to private peace and public position.

In summary, three overriding deficiencies flow from the state of mind and the mythology which grip the states. The first is in orientation—most states are governed in accordance with the rural traditions of an earlier day. The second is in timeliness—the governments of most states are anachronistic; they lack relevance to the urgencies of the modern world. The third is in leadership—state leaders are by confession cautious and tradition-bound, which ill equips them for the tasks of modern government. Governors are less subject to this charge than are legislators, for they represent larger constituencies and therefore are in position to adopt broader views. Unhappily the tone of government is profoundly influenced by the weaker of the two branches. As to the stronger, the 1964–1965 controversy concerning civil rights emphasized anew that leadership is still too frequently a stranger to the office of governor.

CONCLUSION

What has been essayed here is not a systematic critique of state government but rather an evaluation of the states' capacity to react positively and effectively to the demands of a new age. We have concluded that state constitutions are outmoded and inflexible; that the legislatures, identified as the keystone of the democratic arch, are not representative; that resources, partly from deliberate choice, are inadequate; that the atmosphere is not congenial to the embrace of new programs; and that state horizons are severely limited by prevailing mythology. Only with respect to administrative organization was the state's house judged to be in reasonably good order, and by common consent there is ground for improvement there. It must be emphasized that the purpose has been not to judge how well the state does what it does—building roads, running a school system, building and operating state institutions—rather, stress has fallen on the question: How well equipped and how well disposed are the states to assume added responsibilities for urban programs whose natures and dimensions are as yet only vaguely apprehended?

A major reason for concern for the effectiveness of state government resides in the federal duties and responsibilities that fall upon it. Stronger state governments will not, as is sometimes argued, "restore" government to the states by "reversing the trend toward centralization," that is, by weakening the federal system. They will, on the contrary, *strengthen* the federal system by contributing to the more effective practice of cooperative federalism. In an important sense the states may be said to be strong or weak within the context of the federal system. If, as some maintain, federalism has worked but imperfectly in the recent past, a considerable measure of the fault must be placed on the doorstep of the states, which for a variety of reasons have been unable or unwilling to assume the responsibilities properly falling upon them.

This leads to a concluding comment on the role of the states in dealing with the problems of an urban society. The subject may be discussed briefly at two levels. At the first, the states are confused because of the situation they are in. They find themselves suspended somewhere between total agrarianism and total urbanism. When agrarianism alone prevailed, the states could attend to the needs of their people through statewide service programs described in and supported by general legislation. Urbanism is not yet total, hence general legislation is not so neatly applicable as it was half a century ago. To the contrary, the states must identify special urban problems worthy of state action and programs deserving of support. This is a complex and delicate process, one that had only a rude precedent in the earlier and simpler days of an agrarian society. More and more, assistance to the cities, and more particlularly the great cities, takes on the character of helping to meet specialized needs of individual places as identified by special groups. Such assistance is couched in the lofty terms of general legislation, but in truth it requires choices and action of a quite particular character. This is to say, in other words, that the vast new problems of urban America are unique in the experience of the states, which react to them in an impatient and sometimes a truculent manner. Nothing would please the states more than for the cities and their problems to dematerialize into thin air.

At another level the federal government has recognized the complex problems of urban America and has taken a hand in their solution. This confronts the states with the necessity of making decisions on matters they might otherwise ignore, and so adds further to their discomfort. Whose idea was public housing? Or urban renewal? Or pollution abatement? Surely not the states'. Yet the fact that problems exist and that programs have been devised to alleviate them poses a dilemma for the states: Shall they continue to pretend that the problems do not exist, or shall they join in a common attack on the ills of modern society? Answers by the states to this question have been equivocal, as has action spurred by its insistence. The dilemma is charged with consequence for the federal system, for the choices made will affect the balance among federal, state, and city governments in the practice of cooperative federalism.

Many observers believe that the states will prove equal to the challenges of the metropolitan age. The wish doubtless is father to the thought, and the thought perhaps to the hope; but one who allows hope to sire expectation ignores a considerable body of evidence. State readiness and capacity aside, many identify the states as necessary and proper actors in the war on urban ills because of their fundamental role as partners in the federal system. This is not a foregone conclusion, for there is an option to sole reliance on the states, especially on states approaching the issues of urbanism without conviction, enthusiasm, or adequate organization. The option emphasizes increased direct cooperation between the federal government and the cities. It is not an option that commends itself to state devotees, but it nonetheless offers the promise of positive action on metro-urban problems and reasonable support for programs aimed at their alleviation.

4.

Emergence of an Urban Partner

The process by which an urban problem is elevated to national status is long and tortuous, and frequently covers many years. Equally complex are the considerations that enter into the design, structure, and administration of a program to deal with such a problem. The decisions in both instances are developmental and incremental rather than spontaneous and revealed. The forces brought to bear in this development, the parties at interest, the issues debated and resolved, the role of depression and war, the process through which the federal system accommodates to new and changing conditions— these can perhaps be best understood through an examination of the emergence of national policy in a particular program area. The Federal-Aid Airport Program provides a convenient vehicle for such a study.

GOVERNMENT AND CIVIL AVIATION

The national government's interest in aviation goes back more than fifty years, to the time when the War Department first requested bids for the delivery of airplanes. This request was made in December 1907, just four years after the historic flight of the Wright brothers at Kitty Hawk. Five years later the concern of the Navy Department was recognized in a modest appropriation for "experimental work" in aviation. The first transport of mail by air, in 1911, signalized the beginning of interest in that field. The high point of the first decade came with the creation, in 1915, of the

National Advisory Committee for Aeronautics, a research body which symbolized national interest in the new field of aeronautics, even as its successor, the National Aeronautics and Space Administration, does for space travel.[1]

World War I brought with it a tremendous increase in the national interest in aviation. The war suggested the military value of the airplane; it also demonstrated to the satisfaction of many observers that the United States had fallen behind at least three European countries in the development of the new weapon. The consequence of these discoveries was an upsurge of official interest in aeronautics which, in the two decades following the war, produced more than twenty boards and committees with a concern for the nation's role in aviation. These bodies covered an extremely broad range of subjects, among them safety, public regulation of the new industry (particularly of the airlines), airmail service, the provision of facilities, the military implications of the airplane (a continuing preoccupation), and, recurrently, governmental organization to meet the challenge of the air age.[2]

Federal interest in aviation has found legal expression in a series of measures passed by Congress.[3] The first to be mentioned is the Air Commerce Act of 1926 (Public Act 254, 69th Congress, 44 Stat. 568), which signalized the national government's entry into the administration of aviation policy. The act instructed the Secretary of Commerce to promote air commerce, to regulate such com-

[1] The developments of the early years are summarized in Laurence F. Schmeckebier, *The Aeronautics Branch, Department of Commerce: Its History, Activities, and Organization* (Washington, D.C.: The Brookings Institution, 1930), chap. I.

[2] *To Create a Civil Aeronautics Authority:* Hearings before the Committee on Interstate and Foreign Commerce, House of Representatives, 75th Congress, 3rd Session, on H.R. 9738 (March 10–11, 22–25, 29–31, and April 1, 1938). At pp. 377–401 of these Hearings is found a summary of the organization and purpose of and the conclusions reached by each of twenty-two official boards and committees from 1919 through 1937.

[3] There have, of course, been literally scores of federal statutes dealing with aviation, some of them of fundamental importance, many not. Four measures are generally held to have been basic in defining federal policy and providing for its administration. These are the Air Commerce Act (1926), the Civil Aeronautics Act (1938), the Federal Airport Act (1946), and the Federal Aviation Act (1958).

merce and the aircraft engaged in it, and to provide certain aids to air navigation. It was fairly explicit on each of these points, detailing the Secretary's powers and duties at some length. To assist the Secretary in administering its provisions the act provided for an Assistant Secretary of Commerce, who soon came to head the Aeronautics Branch and subsequently the Bureau of Air Commerce. The last was absorbed into the Civil Aeronautics Authority in 1938.

The Air Commerce Act stilled the tumult surrounding the issue of national policy toward aviation; but the respite proved to be temporary, for a rising chorus of dissatisfaction was soon to be heard. The Bureau of Air Commerce, critics charged, was ineffectual, partly because it essayed to deal with only part of the problem, partly because it was "political" in outlook and operation. Three major agencies (the Departments of Commerce and Post Office and the Interstate Commerce Commission) were charged with responsibility for segments of the civil aviation program, with the results usually attendant upon an effort to divide a unified whole. Chief among these results were interdepartmental jealousies, which got in the way of an intelligent approach to the problem.[4] A Federal Aviation Commission, appointed to make a thorough study of aviation and the federal government's relation thereto, in 1935 recommended the creation of an Air Commerce Commission with broad powers to supervise and regulate civil aeronautics.

The answer to these expressions of discontent was the Civil Aeronautics Act of 1938 (Public Act 706, 75th Congress, 3d Session; 52 Stat. 973). The act provided for the concentration of all federal civil aviation concerns in a Civil Aeronautics Authority, to be composed of five members appointed by the President with senatorial consent, and for an Administrator (within the Authority), to be appointed in the same manner. The substantive purposes of the act are disclosed in its declaration of policy (Sec. 2), which provided

[4] *Civil Aviation and Air Transport:* Hearings before a Subcommittee of the Committee on Interstate Commerce, United States Senate, 75th Congress, 3d Session, on S. 3659 (April 6 and 7, 1938). Early in these Hearings, Senator McCarran spoke of "the jealousies that exist under the interdepartmental conditions here in Washington, . . ." and Senator Truman (presiding) interceded to remark: "That has been our great difficulty, the jealousies between departments" (p. 8).

that the Authority should encourage the development of an air transportation system "properly adapted to the present and future needs of the foreign and domestic commerce of the United States . . ."; regulate air transportation in a way calculated to promote safety, sound economic conditions, competition, and good relations among the air carriers; foster the growth of an adequate, economical, and effective air transportation service at reasonable charges; and encourage and develop civil aeronautics.

Substance apart, the Civil Aeronautics Act was significant for a number of reasons. It constituted a long step toward maturity for federal policy regarding civil aviation. National policy was not yet firm in some important areas, but at any rate the country had come to grips with and resolved some basic issues. Most important, it had demonstrated its intent to deal positively with civil aeronautics, and to that end had established an independent agency in which were concentrated the civil aviation functions of the government. No matter that the new agency was soon to lose its separate status through transfer to the Department of Commerce; never was it to lose its place as the focal point of national concern for civil aviation. The act was further significant because it represented the last deliberate look that Congress would be able to give the subject for some years. Before the government would find it possible to return to the problems of civil aviation, the developments of defense and then of war would have changed drastically the perspective on the whole field.

THE ISSUE OF FEDERAL AID

One policy issue of the greatest importance to which the Civil Aeronautics Act gave attention concerned the role to be played by the national government in the development of airway and airport facilities. The fundamental importance of the airport for air navigation had long been recognized, yet both President and Congress had consistently shied away from any assumption of responsibility for airport development by the federal government. The provision of landing facilities by tradition had been either a municipal or a commercial function, and there was no disposition on the part of national leaders to interfere with the established pattern. Thus the Air Commerce Act of 1926 [in Sec. 5, Para. (b)] authorized the Secretary of Commerce "to establish, operate, and maintain along such airways all necessary air navigation facilities *except airports* . . ." (emphasis supplied). This phrase came to symbolize an ideological commitment to federal aviation policy which remained paramount in congressional consideration of the subject for many years. It is not strange, therefore, that House Resolution 9738, which (as amended) was passed in 1938 as the Civil Aeronautics Act, contained the by now familiar exception: Section 302 proposed to give to the Civil Aeronautics Authority the power "to establish, operate, and maintain along such airways all necessary air navigation facilities, except airports used . . . for commercial purposes. . . ."

The hearings on H.R. 9738 conducted by the House Committee on Interstate and Foreign Commerce brought out quite clearly the nature of the conflict. A variety of witnesses, among whom the spokesmen of the cities were perhaps most vocal, favored elimination of the controverted phrase. The confessed poverty of the cities and the national interest in sound air navigation facilities enabled the urban representatives to make a strong plea for federal participation in airport development. A resolution adopted by the United States Conference of Mayors and introduced into the record by its executive director called for "a permanent program of federal financial cooperation in the construction, improvement, development, and expansion of publicly owned airports, . . ." A document filed by the director of the American Municipal Association in behalf of that body's executive committee summarized the position of the cities in these words:

1. That airports, to many cities, and especially to the larger centers, are a necessity to meet present-day transportation needs, although they have no longer any particular value as a community advertisement.
2. That a very large proportion of traffic, both passenger and freight, of municipal airports is interstate in character.
3. There is an immediate necessity for a uniform planning and development of airports.
4. Works Progress Administration relief labor has been and can

be effectively used in the development of airports. Proper planning will allow continuance of such projects.

5. Airports, while financed locally, are . . . interstate and national in character, but . . . no power exists by which local governments can. create and derive any revenue from the interstate business carried on through airports.

6. Airports have important military significance and form an indispensable part of the system of national and State defense schemes.

7. While the States should have the local supervision and policing of air transportation and the designing, construction, maintenance, and operation of airports, yet it is imperative that the Federal Government . . . make more definite and complete plans to which the States and their municipalities may gear their plans.

8. The Federal Government should prescribe a system of national civil airways and airports, just as it prescribed and plotted a system of Federal highways, in order that the States and cities may plan their State systems of airways and airports with reference to Federal needs and requirements: . . .[5]

A separate resolution on airports approved by the AMA and filed for the record urged adoption of a system of federal aid for municipal airport development. Yet another resolution, adopted by a National Airport Conference, called specifically for elimination of the words "except airports."

The issue at stake was nothing less than that of active financial participation by the federal government in a new and rapidly expanding field. It was, of course, generally recognized. The Assistant General Counsel of the Treasury Department, Clinton M. Hester, who was to become the Administrator under the Civil Aeronautics Act, summarized the issue quite succinctly. If you delete the words "except airports," he said, you will commit the federal government to a nationwide program of airport construction that might involve the expenditure of hundreds of millions of dollars.[6]

The House committee, accepting the challenge, voted to strike the restrictive phrase. A conference committee, appointed subsequently to resolve the differences between the House and the Senate, accepted the recommendation of the House committee, and so, ultimately, did the two houses. Section 302(a) of the Civil Aeronautics

[5] *To Create a Civil Aeronautics Authority, op. cit.*, pp. 106–124. Paragraphs quoted at p. 107.
[6] *Ibid.*, pp. 424–425.

Act reads, in part: "The Administrator is empowered . . . to acquire, establish, operate, and maintain along such airways all necessary air navigation facilities. . . ." Thus did Congress and the President, through his signature, set a course that was to eventuate in an active federal-aid program.

The strategy of those who favored federal aid had been to seek two goals: the elimination of the restrictive clause, and the authorization of an official survey to determine the status and needs of air navigation so as to arrive at recommendations regarding the effectuation of the national interest in the field of civil aeronautics. The executive director of the United States Conference of Mayors proposed an amendment to the House bill which his organization felt would represent a constructive approach to "the airport problem that is now confronting the various communities throughout the country." The proposed amendment provided for a comprehensive field survey and set forth in specific terms the purposes it should seek to achieve. The committee adopted the recommendation, which survived subsequent steps in the legislative process to find a place in the Civil Aeronautics Act. Section 302(c) of the act states:

> The Authority shall, through the Administrator, make a field survey of the existing system of airports and shall present to the Congress not later than February 1, 1939, definite recommendations (1) as to whether the Federal Government should participate in the construction, improvement, development, operation, or maintenance of a national system of airports, and (2) if Federal participation is recommended, the extent to which, and the manner in which, the Federal Government shall so participate.

Pursuant to this directive, the Administrator proceeded to launch a survey of the nation's airport system. His report, which was transmitted to the Speaker of the House of Representatives on March 23, 1939, constituted not only an inventory and appraisal of the existing system but also an analysis of needs and of ways and means of meeting those needs. The report examined the economic and social importance of air transportation, the contribution of an effective system of air navigation to the nation's commerce, the place of civil aeronautics in national defense, the importance of a national system of airports for the training of pilots, and the contribution that a vigorous civil aviation enterprise would make to the aircraft industry. In summary, the conclusions regarding federal participation in the development of an airport system were:

1. Development and maintenance of an adequate system of airports and seaplane bases should be recognized in principle as a matter of national concern.

2. Such a system should be regarded, under certain conditions, as a proper object of Federal expenditure.

3. At such times as the national policy includes the making of grants to local units of government for public-works purposes, or any work-relief activity, a proportion of the funds involved should be allocated to airport purposes.

4. Whenever emergency public-works programs may be terminated; or when such programs may be curtailed to a degree not enabling adequate development to continue; or when the Congress for other reasons may determine, Federal assistance for airports should be continued through annual appropriations for that purpose. . . .[7]

From the emphasis on public-works and work-relief activities, it is clear that the Civil Aeronautics Authority did not purpose to rush pell-mell into the uncharted sea of federal aid for airport construction. Nevertheless the report did discuss "The Nature of a National Plan." It proposed an "extended plan" to include 3,500 airports, and classified the airports and set down their characteristics in some detail; it also recommended active federal participation in the execution of the plan.

Meanwhile history was running against those who opposed a program of federal aid, and for reasons not directly related to the merits of the controversy. Prior to 1933, municipal and commercial sources had accounted, almost equally, for more than 97 per cent of all capital expenditures on civil airports and landing areas. With the coming of the depression these springs dried up, the latter (private or commercial financing) never to flow again. Fortunately a substitute source of financing was found in the various federal work-relief and public-works programs, which from 1933 to 1938 provided the

[7] *Airport Survey:* Letter from the Civil Aeronautics Authority Transmitting Recommendations as to the Desirability of Federal Participation in the Construction, Improvement, Development, Operation, and Maintenance of a National System of Airports (76th Congress, 1st Session, House Document No. 245, 1939). Paragraphs quoted at p. 129.

resources for 77 per cent of all capital expenditures on civil airports. Of the remainder, the cities contributed three-fourths. State expenditures never at any time exceeded 2 per cent of the total. The depression years therefore witnessed the launching of a vigorous program of federal participation in airport development. It is not without reason that the Civil Aeronautics Authority later observed that "1933 marks the greatest of all changes in Federal airport policy."[8]

The onset of the defense program, which distracted attention from civil aviation as such, nevertheless proved a boon to the emerging airport program; for if the construction of airports could not be justified in the name of civil air navigation in a time of national crisis, it could readily be sustained as part of the defense (and presently the war) effort. Hence work on civil airports went right along with vigorous federal support, not only without interruption but also with increased intensity. A report requested of the Civil Aeronautics Administration by a House resolution, which was transmitted November 28, 1944, summarized wartime developments.[9] So also did a statement made by an official of the Civil Aeronautics Administration before the House Committee on Interstate and Foreign Commerce on May 22, 1945.[10] These documents reveal that federal expenditures for civil aviation during the war years followed two main channels. First, the public works programs, and particularly that vested in the Works Progress/Work Projects Administration, remained active. Second, Congress determined upon a course of civil airport development by direct appropriation, with the CAA as the administrative agency; and a vigorous construction program emerged from this decision.

[8] *Ibid.,* p. 12. The figures in this paragraph are summarized from Table 1, p. 13.

[9] *National Airport Plan:* Letter from the Acting Secretary of Commerce Transmitting a Report of a Survey of the Need for a System of Airports and Landing Areas Throughout the United States (78th Congress, 2d Session, House Document No. 807, 1945), pp. 16–20.

[10] *Legislative History of the Federal Airport Act* (Public Law 377, 79th Congress, Chapter 251, 2d Session), vol. Two, *House Action* (April 1948), pp. 69–71. This document comprises two volumes: Volume One, *Senate Action,* and Volume Two, *House Action.* It provides a detailed record of congressional action on the Federal Airport Act.

Table 3 presents a summary of federal expenditures for civil airport development during the depression and the defense/war years. It indicates that the national government's investment for this period (some fourteen years) totaled almost $800 million. Thus did the President and Congress, responding first to the need for depression spending and second to the demands of the defense and subsequently the war effort, launch and implement a new program calling for the development of civil airports by federal action. The figures indicate that the program was a substantial one; Senator

**Table 3. Federal Expenditures for Development of
Civil Airports, 1933–1947**

Civil Works Administration, November 1933–June 1934	$ 15,222,372
Federal Emergency Relief Agency, May 1933–June 1938	17,649,853
Public Works Administration, May 1933–June 1943	28,849,672
Works Progress Administration, May 1935–July 1939 ⎱	331,584,806
Work Projects Administration, July 1939–December 1942 ⎰	
Development Landing Areas—National Defense, December 1940–1947	383,031,875
Development Civil Landing Areas, September 1944	9,513,995
Public Roads Administration	10,328,000
Total	$796,180,573

Source: Records of the Airports Service, Federal Aviation Agency.

McCarran, indeed, characterized its works as "the greatest system of civil airports in the world." It was accomplished almost entirely through grants to the cities and direct construction by national agencies. By the end of the war, then, an active if rough-hewn federal-aid airport program had come into being. That it was the legatee of crisis in no wise detracted from its strength or value as a going concern, or from public expectation that it would be continued. The precedent had been set.

As the war passed its critical phase and prospects appeared for a reasonably early return of peace, those interested in civil aviation turned their thoughts to the federal-aid program suggested but not explicated in the Civil Aeronautics Act. Considerable progress in the construction and improvement of airports had been made under the public works and the defense/war programs; but the time was now approaching when civil airport development could be considered on its merits rather than as an antidote to depression or an arm of the war effort. The favorable climate resulted in the introduction into Congress of no fewer than half a dozen bills during the first half of 1945. Although differing in detail, they were uniform in their purpose. This was, in basic terms, to provide for a program of federal aid for the improvement and construction of public airports. The appropriate committees conducted hearings and took extensive testimony on these measures during the spring and early summer of 1945. S. 2 and S. 34 emerged as the key bills in the Senate; H.R. 3615 (a redraft of H.R. 3170, which was the subject of most of the committee hearings) provided the basis for final House action.

The testimony offered at the hearings turned first on the desirability of a program of federal aid for public airport development. The witnesses before both Senate and House committees were all but unanimous in their endorsement of such a program. Specifically, thirty-four witnesses representing a wide variety of interests, private as well as public, appeared before the Senate Subcommittee on Aviation of the Committee on Commerce; and they took a uniformly favorable view of the stated purpose of the bills under discussion.[11] Similarly in the House, a member of the Committee on Interstate and Foreign Commerce reported that "every witness appearing before the committee on this legislation was in favor of the Federal-aid airport . . . program which [it] authorizes."[12] In this environment the committees found little difficulty in recommending to the Congress that it take positive steps to implement the policy projected in the Civil Aeronautics Act and endorsed in particular by the Airport Survey. The Federal Airport Act, passed shortly, incorporated the recommendation, thus embracing the principle of federal aid in civil airport development as national policy.

[11] See the "Digest of Testimony on S. 2 and S. 34," *ibid.*, vol. One, pp. 449–470. Both bills provided for federal aid for public airport development.
[12] *Ibid.*, vol. Two, p. 645.

THE RECIPIENT GOVERNMENT DILEMMA

Once the policy of federal aid in public airport development had been agreed upon, there remained the question of the government with which the federal agency should deal in administering the grant-in-aid program. This proved to be much more controversial than the basic issue of federal support. In briefest terms, the question was whether the federal government should deal with the states or with the cities direct in allocating grant funds. To put the problem in simple terms, however, is not to suggest that it was susceptible of a simple solution; for contained in the state-city conflict is a basic dilemma of the federal-aid airport program. This dilemma was the cause of sharp disagreement in what otherwise might have been a harmonious, perhaps even a routine, procedure.

The Two Positions. The cause of states' rights received its most vigorous defense at the hands of Governor Herbert B. Maw, of Utah, who testified before the Senate Subcommittee on Aviation of the Committee on Commerce as spokesman for the Governors' Conference and (inferentially) the Council of State Governments.[13] Governor Maw began with the assertion that the states favored the proposed federal-aid program and that they were willing to do whatever was required, by way either of new legislation or of appropriation, to make it a success. The first step in this direction, he felt, was to recognize the new program as a federal-state partnership; for the states alone were capable of performing the opposite-number services required by a system of federal aid. The reasons outlined by Maw for going through the states may be summarized thus:

1. The municipalities will emerge from the war in bad financial condition and will require the assistance of the states, whose broader taxing powers will give them an advantage in dealing with the difficult postwar problems which lie ahead.

2. The states have a further advantage over the municipalities in the matter of public-works personnel, equipment, and facilities. They are accustomed to handling the technical problems which airport development will involve.

[13] The position of the states was generally associated with that of states' rights. Governor Maw's testimony appears in *ibid.*, vol. One, pp. 373–388.

3. Channeling the grant program through the states would make easier the coordination of all airport programs within a state.

4. The states will be expected to render certain services and (probably) to make certain payments in connection with the new program, and ought therefore to be administratively responsible for it.

5. Only the states would be able to bring about cooperation between neighboring (and possibly disputing) municipalities.

6. The states have had long experience in federal-aid programs in such fields as highways, agriculture, public health, vocational education, and social security.

7. The federal-state pattern has been satisfactory and successful in other grant-in-aid programs, and there is no reason for deserting it in the case of the proposed airport program. The federal-aid highway program is closely analogous to the airport program; it points the way to a sound administrative arrangement.

Coincidentally, Governor Maw spoke against adoption of a direct federal-city pattern. The grounds given, briefly, were these:

1. Such a system would encourage the cities to compete with each other for federal aid.

2. Because of the magnitude of the proposed program and the enthusiasm for it, the municipalities would be stimulated to undertake "extravagant projects" which would weigh heavily on them in the years to come.

3. The federal Administrator would be required to negotiate separately with hundreds of municipalities. He would not be equipped to do this, and in any event he could not do it as well as the states.

The witness took occasion to observe that the national airport plan was not a very satisfactory document, partly if not largely because in drafting it the Administrator had relied too heavily on federal employees and the cities and too little on the states.

Governor Maw's appearance was the more impressive because he was accompanied by four other members of the executive committee of the Governor's Conference. These were the Governors of Alabama, Maryland, Nebraska, and Pennsylvania, who corroborated Maw's views. Further to authenticate the states' rights position, telegrams were entered into the record from forty-four governors, all but one of whom gave these views hearty endorsement.

Those who favored granting federal aid direct to the cities were similarly vigorous and articulate. The arguments for the federal-city pattern were, in summary, these:

1. An airport is peculiarly an urban facility.

2. Most airport construction has been under the direction of the cities. They are therefore quite familiar with the special problems involved, and are well equipped through experience to handle such problems.

3. The states have taken very little interest in airport development, and as a consequence have had quite limited experience in this field.

4. Interposition of the states between the federal government and the cities in airport development would constitute a serious blow at municipal home rule.

5. The states are not equipped to participate effectively in an airport development program. Administratively their aeronautic agencies are weak and ill-supported; financially they have spent almost no money on airport development, and there is little promise that they will spend more. Some states simply are not interested in the development of municipal airports and have so stated.

6. Adoption of the federal-state formula would entail a considerable delay while the states tooled themselves up to do the new job.

7. Some states might elect not to participate in the program, in which case their cities would find themselves without an effective channel for receipt of federal aid.

8. The analogy between federal aid for airport development and federal aid for highway construction is not valid, since airways and highways are completely different in their requirements for and uses of properties and facilities.

9. The relations between the Civil Aeronautics Administration and the cities have been entirely satisfactory, and no sound case has been made for a change.

10. Making a national airport plan is unmistakably a job for the federal government; it cannot be done piecemeal by the simple

process of assembling forty-eight state plans, as urged by some of the states' rights advocates.

The most ardent proponents of a federal-city arrangement were the municipalities. The representative of the American Municipal Association, appearing before the House Committee on Interstate and Foreign Commerce, testified in judicious terms, noting that some municipalities preferred direct relations with the federal government while others would be satisfied to go through the states. He reported nevertheless that the cities, on balance, favored a direct relationship:

> It is . . . evident that the cities of a few States favor the Federal-State-municipal relationship while a greater majority desire direct relationship with the CAA. The cities which are in favor of channeling funds through State agencies are in States which over a period of years have had well established, efficient State airport agencies. These States, however, are in the minority.[14]

The AMA witness before the Senate Subcommittee on Aviation of the Committee on Commerce was if anything even more equivocal, though in the end he came to the same point. The cities, as creatures of the states, were of course willing to have the federal-aid money go through the states where required by state law, but they did not wish the federal statute to stipulate that procedure. He expressed the hope that, in any event, Congress would not deny the cities access to the federal government.

The spokesmen of the large cities were not so circumspect. Mayor LaGuardia, of New York City, representing the United States Conference of Mayors before the House committee, stated his position clearly in these words: "All I have to say is that if we, the cities, are paying the freight and providing the funds out of local revenues, there is no place in the picture for any intermediary State agency." LaGuardia filed a document for the record which indicated that, to May 29, 1945, forty states had made no appropriations for airports. Of the eight states that had expressed their intention to give financial support to airport development, one had an appropria-

---

[14] *Ibid.*, vol. Two, p. 198. The American Municipal Association, though incorporating through its member-state leagues most of the large cities, nevertheless is regarded primarily as the spokesman of cities of medium size and smaller.

tion under consideration at the time and two had appropriated money to aeronautics commissions which in turn might contribute (quite modestly) to airport development. Only five states—Michigan, Minnesota, Pennsylvania, Utah, and Virginia—had made actual appropriations for the construction and improvement of airports, and the amount appropriated reached a total of no more than $7.5 million. Mayor LaGuardia in his testimony emphasized what seemed to him the palpable lack of state interest in airports, though before he finished he repeated most of the arguments noted above. In summarizing his views, he said bluntly, "I want to come to Washington to do business. I do not want to go to Albany to do business and I do not think my colleague, Mayor Kelly, of Chicago, wants to go to Springfield." As if in refrain, Mayor Kelly, who followed Mayor LaGuardia as a witness, gave full corroboration to the latter's testimony.[15]

The nature of the dispute was indicated by the principal parties to it. The Council of State Governments strongly supported the pattern of federal-state relations which had prevailed almost uniformly in the administration of federal grant-in-aid programs until 1932. The United States Conference of Mayors (representing the large cities) argued with equal vigor for explicit statutory endorsement of the practice of direct federal-city relations which had expanded greatly with the depression and had continued during the war years.[16] The argument in effect pitted the states against the large cities; the issue indeed was squarely joined in these terms. Congressional committee members considering the various bills confessed more than once that their principal difficulty lay in reconciling the opposing views of the states and the cities.

Congressional Action and Reaction. The provisions of the several bills at various stages of congressional action will indicate both the nature of the problem and the progress of congressional

[15] *Ibid.*, vol. Two, pp. 245–294 *passim*. Mayor LaGuardia was president of the United States Conference of Mayors, Mayor Kelly was vice president. The mayors received a strong assist in the form of a vigorous statement favoring the federal-city pattern by the president of the National Institute of Municipal Law Officers.

[16] The positions attributed to the states and the cities are made explicit in *ibid.*, vol. One, p. 460.

thinking regarding it. Two bills were introduced in the Senate the same day (January 6, 1945); they were S. 2, by Senator McCarran, and S. 34, by Senator Bailey. Both measures provided for a federal-aid airport program, and both accepted the Civil Aeronautics Administration recommendation that the program be divided into two parts, one urban, the other state. The bills differed radically, however, with respect to the manner of handling and the relative weight to be given the two programs. S. 2 would have included in the urban program class 3, 4, and 5 airports, thus limiting the state program to classes 1 and 2.[17] S. 34 drew the line between the state program and the urban program in such fashion as to include both larger airports and a larger number of airports in the state program. It proposed to allot to the state program all airports of classes 1, 2, and 3, placing in the urban program airports of classes 4 and 5. Moreover, S. 34 proposed to allocate federal grant moneys 75 per cent to the state program, 25 per cent to the urban program. This placed it in contrast with S. 2, which proposed to divide federal funds on a 50–50 basis. The two bills clearly represented a sharp difference in philosophy: S. 2 sought to elevate the cities, whereas S. 34 emphasized the role of the states.

Spokesmen of the Civil Aeronautics Administration, in their testimony on the bills before the Senate subcommittee, in effect expressed a preference for S. 34 with respect to the division between state and urban programs. Pointing out that the airports in classes 4 and 5 would be restricted to the larger cities and would number only 316 all told, a CAA official said, "I believe we prefer to deal with class 4 and 5 directly with the cities and the rest with the States."[18] The Senate Committee on Commerce, persuaded by this and other like testimony, incorporated CAA thinking into the bill reported to the Senate. The Committee bill, reported as S. 2, allo-

[17] The classification of airports employed was developed by the CAA in a bulletin titled *Airport Design* and dated April 1, 1944. Classes 1, 2, and 3 comprised the smaller airports, with landing strips up to 4,700 feet in length; classes 4 and 5 included the larger airports, with landing strips 4,700 feet and over in length. Generally speaking, class 4 and 5 airports were found in cities of 100,000 and over. The ten-year work program developed by the CAA included 316 airports of classes 4 and 5.

[18] *Legislative History of the Federal Airport Act, op. cit.,* vol. One, p. 389.

cated airports of classes 1, 2, and 3 (the smaller airports) to the state program, airports of classes 4 and 5 (the larger airports) to the urban program. Striking a middle ground between the original allocation proposal of S. 2 and that of S. 34, the bill stipulated that not more than 35 per cent of any federal appropriation might be dedicated to the urban program, with the remainder to be available for the state program [Secs. 5, 7(b)]. The measure provided further (in Sec. 4) that "the (CAA) Administrator is . . . authorized, within the limits of available appropriations made therefor by the Congress, to make grants of funds to the States, their political subdivisions, and other non-Federal public agencies for the development of public airports. . . ." In reporting the bill, Senator McCarran presented it as "a compromise between those who advocate an airport program on a Federal-State basis and those who support the Federal-city basis. . . ."[19]

The Senate devoted three days to debate on S. 2. Its major critic was Senator Brewster, who early made clear his opposition to the bill as reported. "The chief issue," he stated, "deals with the question whether in the allocation of the Federal funds the channeling shall be through a state agency or directly to a municipality." The Council of State Governments, he noted, is concerned lest the principle recommended by the committee, if endorsed by the Senate, result in further serious encroachment on state responsibility. The idea that the cities should come, or should be encouraged to come, to Washington with their problems strikes at the very foundation of the federal system, he continued; clearly any dealings which the cities and the federal government may find it necessary to have with each other must be conducted through the states if the American system is to be preserved.[20]

To give bite to his position, Senator Brewster introduced an amendment to require that all federal grants for airport development be channeled through state agencies; the sole purpose of the amendment, as stated by its author, was "to determine the issue

---

[19] *Ibid.*, vol. One, p. 445.

[20] The central ideas summarized here appear in *ibid.*, vol. One, pp. 529 and 531, quotation at p. 527. Senator Brewster's views in opposition to and Senator McCarran's in support of the bill are elaborated at length.

between the States and the city authorities. . . ."[21] Senator Mc-
Carran defended the committee's formula stoutly, noting that it
had been arrived at over a long period and that it represented a
carefully constructed compromise between two strongly held and
vigorously defended views. Adoption of the Brewster amendment,
he concluded, would mean "the complete destruction of the philosophy of the bill."[22] Senator Saltonstall, speaking in support of the
amendment, sought to soften its impact through a temperate interpretation, but his efforts failed to mollify the partisans of the bill
as reported by the committee. The amendment nevertheless prevailed, with 40 senators favoring, 33 opposing, and 23 not voting.
It may not be without significance that its chief proponents, Senators
Brewster and Saltonstall, were former governors.

The final version of S. 2 as passed by the Senate therefore provided simply (in Sec. 4) that "the Administrator is . . . authorized,
within the limits of available appropriations made therefor by the
Congress, to make grants of funds to the States for the development
of public airports. . . ." Amended Sec. 7 dropped the concept of
urban as distinguished from state program, but retained for purposes of fund allocation the distinction based on airport size. Of the
federal funds available for grants for any fiscal year, 65 per cent was
to be apportioned among the state airport agencies for the development of class 3 and smaller airports; 35 per cent was to be apportioned, *also among state airport agencies,* for the development of
class 4 and larger airports in urban areas. The Senate thus rejected
the compromise report of its Committee on Commerce, adopting un-
equivocally the states' rights view on the all-important issue of
channeling federal funds.

States' rights fared less well in the House of Representatives.
The basic House bill, introduced as H.R. 3170, provided [in Sec.
5(b)] that, for each fiscal year, the Administrator should apportion
among the several states 75 per cent of all federal funds available
for that year, reserving the remaining 25 per cent for grants-in-aid
deemed "most appropriate for carrying out the national airport
plan" without regard for allocation among the states. It also stipu-

21 *Ibid.*, vol. One, p. 563.
22 *Ibid.*, vol. One, p. 546.

lated, in a key policy determination [Sec. 6(a)], that any non-federal public agency might submit a project application. Equally significant with these positive provisions was the bill's omission of mention of state airport agencies in connection with fund apportionment and project sponsorship. Clearly the measure meant to allow for such federal-city relations as the prospective program might naturally and conveniently lead to.

The history of H.R. 3170 in the House was generally comparable with that of S. 2 in the Senate. The Committee on Interstate and Foreign Commerce conducted exhaustive hearings, during which the issue of federal-state versus federal-city relations was examined in detail. Questions asked of the witnesses likewise emphasized this problem. Many of those appearing before House and Senate committees were identical, which doubtless accounts for a certain sameness in the testimony.

Debate was reserved largely for H.R. 3615, a redraft of the initial bill prepared after hearings and reported to the Committee of the Whole House on the State of the Union. The revised measure, which did not differ in essentials from the bill it superseded, provoked vigorous debate, even as did S. 2 and S. 34 in the Senate. Senator Brewster's counterpart in the House turned out to be Congressman Howell (Illinois), who introduced an amendment "aimed specifically at channeling funds provided for under this national airport development plan through the State aviation agencies." The arguments of Mr. Howell and his supporters prevailed in the Committee of the Whole, which accepted the amendment over the energetic opposition of Congressmen Lea (California) and Bulwinkle (North Carolina), who led the fight for the reporting committee. At the House vote stage the bill's managers rallied their forces to bring about the rejection of the Howell amendment, notwithstanding the earlier favorable vote in the Committee of the Whole. The way to rejection had been paved by a conciliatory amendment, proposed by Congressman Bulwinkle and accepted by the Committee of the Whole, which provided that no state or local project application not in conformity with state law would be deemed to be authorized by the act. Finally, H.R. 3615, as reported originally by the Committee on Interstate and Foreign Commerce, passed without substantial amendment of its critical provisions.[23]

THE CRYSTALLIZATION OF POLICY

S. 2 was approved by the Senate on September 12, 1945, and was sent to the House for consideration. Action there took the form of passage of the House bill as an amendment to the Senate measure. Soon after the House vote (on October 26, 1945), S. 2, as passed by the Senate and amended by the House, went to conference. If the testimony of members of the conference committee is to be accepted, the discussion in that body was repetitious and tedious in the extreme. It was also arduous, covering as it did a series of meetings held intermittently over a period of five months. The principal issue remained the manner of channeling federal funds. Other problems occasioned no sharp differences, but on this one question there appeared to be no acceptable compromise position between the stand taken by the Senate and that embraced by the House.

The conference report revealed that in truth no middle ground had been found; for the bill brought before the two bodies was essentially the House amendment to S. 2—that is, in effect, H.R. 3615. Some minor modifications had been made in conference, but on the basic issues the House conferees had stood firm and those from the Senate had retreated. On the central question of states versus cities as the recipients of federal grants, the conference bill explicitly endorsed the House position that any public agency might make application direct for a federal grant for the development of a public airport.

The reception accorded the conference bill in the two houses was what might have been expected. In the Senate, Senators Brewster and Saltonstall were quite unhappy and did what they could to bring about rejection of the bill. The thinly veiled charge of a sellout

---

[23] *Ibid.*, vol. Two, p. 749. The vote was 279 for and 82 against, with 70 not voting. The history of the states' rights amendments (the Howell amendment in fact consisted of several individual amendments, all, however, designed to achieve one end) is detailed on pp. 680–748. Congressman Howell's quoted statement appears at p. 680.

by Senate conferees brought the rejoinder from Senator McCarran that the bill not only was the best obtainable from the committee but also was a very good bill. The final Senate vote was 49 favorable, 32 opposed.[24] In the House, Representatives Bulwinkle, Lea, and Wolverton led the measure to victory the more easily because that body was asked to do little more than ratify a favorable vote previously recorded. Congressman Howell remained unsatisfied, but his was a minority voice. The House approved the bill by a final vote of 140 for, 81 against.[25]

The Federal Airport Act was approved by the President on May 13, 1946 (Public Law 377, 79th Congress, Chapter 251, 2d Session; 60 Stat. 170). This was the third major federal law dealing with civil aviation passed to that date, and it is, perhaps, the most important of the three. It builds on the organizational structure established under the Civil Aeronautics Act, hence it minimizes the subject of administration in favor of emphasis on a system of federal aid for the development of public airports. The major policy decisions reflected by the act were:

1. The Administrator of Civil Aeronautics is directed to prepare and to revise annually a national plan for the development of public airports.

2. In order to bring into being a nationwide system of public airports adequate to meet the needs of civil aviation, and in pursuance of the national plan, there is established a system of federal-aid grants for the development of public airports.

3. Seventy-five per cent of any particular appropriation for airport development shall be apportioned by the Administrator among the several states. All moneys appropriated and not so apportioned shall be regarded as a discretionary fund, and shall be allocated by the Administrator to approved projects without regard for location.

4. Any public agency, or two or more public agencies acting jointly, may (under stipulated conditions) submit to the Administrator a project application. Tender of an offer of aid by the Ad-

---

[24] *Ibid.*, vol. One, p. 643. Senate debate on the conference bill may be found on pp. 625–643.

[25] *Ibid.*, vol. Two, p. 783. House debate on the conference bill appears on pp. 773–783.

ministrator and acceptance by the sponsor shall constitute a grant agreement between the United States and the sponsor.

5. The Administrator is required to submit his recommendations of projects for the development of class 4 and larger airports to the Congress each year for prior authorization, and no grants may be made for such projects unless so authorized.

6. The federal contribution is fixed at 50 per cent of the allowable project costs for any project involving a class 3 or smaller airport; for class 4 and larger airport projects, the Administrator may fix the federal contribution at a figure not to exceed 50 per cent of the allowable project costs.

7. The Administrator is given broad powers to set standards, inspect, and pass on the acceptability of the work done.

The central problem addressed by Congress in the deliberations detailed here was the delineation of national policy in the new, rapidly growing, and obviously important field of air transport. The first basic decision was that which called for active federal participation in the field. The second, by emphasizing the national character of aviation, pointed inescapably to the need for a national policy. The third decision pertained to policy content. It did not prove difficult, as the argument took form and thinking crystallized, to conclude that the federal government must assume responsibility both for a national plan for the development of public airports and for financial support of a program designed to bring a national system of airports into being. The federal grant-in-aid program was the logical consequence of this line of reasoning.

The fourth major decision occasioned sharper and more prolonged debate than all the others combined, for it concerned an issue close to the core of the federal system. By tradition and by historic practice the national government was propelled toward the states in seeking a means to implement the new grant-in-aid program. The federal-state highway program, among others, was a useful exhibit for those favoring the federal-state channel. At the same time, the experience of the period 1932–1946 suggested the availability of an alternative that might offer advantages over the traditional arrangement. The "greatest system of airports in the world" was the product of a development in federalism that featured direct relations between the national government and the cities. The cities had played a major role in bringing the nation's airport system into being, whereas the states' contribution had been negligible. If ever a facility might be said to be peculiarly urban in nature, it was the airport. In principle, the states were concerned with the development of public airports; in practice, to 1946 they had spent little money on airports and appeared far from ready to carry the other end of the federal grant-in-aid stick.

Congress heard the states' rights argument, which was presented forcefully and at length, then turned to the cities as a basic partner of the national government in the new federal-aid airport program. It rejected the stipulation that federal grants must go through a state agency in favor of the provision that any public agency (within defined limits) might serve as the sponsor of an airport development project and might negotiate and contract direct with the federal government. Recognizing that, in the end, the states were sovereign over all local units, including the cities, Congress included in the act [as Sec. 9(b)] a proviso which made obeisance toward the states: "Nothing in this Act shall authorize the submission of a project application by any municipality or other public agency which is subject to the law of any State if the submission of such project application by such municipality or other public agency is prohibited by the law of such State." Those who favored the states' rights view complained that this added nothing to what everybody knew and accepted already as an elementary principle of constitutional law, but it was as much as Congress was willing to say on the subject. The decision for dealing with the cities direct in the absence of a positive state prohibition was a firm one.

The policy hammered out in the continuing crisis of depression, defense, and war, and ratified by the Federal Airport Act in 1946, remains in effect almost twenty years later. The expectation entertained by some that the states would rush to take action establishing aviation agencies and requiring federal-aid funds to be channeled through them has failed of realization. Today there are in fact active aviation agencies in fewer than half the states. This suggests that aviation has not been found an especially rewarding area for state activity. Some states do indeed require the channeling of federal-aid airport funds through agencies established by them, but the requirement varies widely in its effect. At one extreme the state agency merely receives the federal check, endorses it, and sends it along to the sponsor. At the other, a few states actually assert their legal prerogative to play an active role in the federal-aid process; but very few participate to the extent of making significant appropriations for airport development. With regard to the major airports the federal government and the cities remain the principal partners in the federal-aid program, whose true nature is revealed by the fact that 85 per cent of all federal airport aid goes for projects in the larger cities, and by the further fact that respecting virtually all such projects the sponsor deals direct with the Federal Aviation Agency.

In the important field of airport development the relations of convenience that grew up between the cities and the federal government in days of crisis thus were confirmed subsequently as deliberate policy. Congressional insistence on maintaining and systematizing these relations stemmed from three primary considerations. First, there is evidence that Congress desired to maintain close control over the federal-aid airport program, particularly as it involved the larger cities. Such evidence appears most overtly in the provision for congressional authorization of projects involving the larger airports, a stipulation for which long-established practice with respect to river and harbor projects furnished ample precedent. In recognizing the cities as partners with the federal government, Congress thus incidentally but effectively maximized its own role. Second, the federal-city arrangement had worked well since 1932 and no compelling reason was found to abandon it. Third, airport development is an activity that lends itself peculiarly to municipal endeavor. The city's concern is primary, the state's secondary. Air traffic may be called a discontinuous operation—it makes its physical presence felt only at the moment of landing and take-off; that is, only when it employs the facilities of an airport. What happens between airports is of course highly important, but it is also largely intangible; further, it is a matter for which the federal government has assumed primary responsibility. It would appear that a case for direct federal-city relations could be made with respect to any federal-aid program that is of like significance for the cities and is similarly discontinuous. The primary elements in the forging of direct programmatic relations between the federal government and the cities, therefore, would seem to be centrality of urban impact, discontinuity, and absence of demonstrated state concern.

5.

The Expanded Partnership: Nature

By tradition the American federal system rests upon two partners, the nation and the states. By practice the system has been modified to accommodate a third partner, the cities. A number of factors have figured in this modification. The states have been loath to grapple with urban problems, particularly the vast and complex problems of a volatile metro-society. The cities for over a hundred years have played a more vigorous role in the federal system than has been commonly understood. Events during the past three decades have brought the developing role of the cities into public notice. There is overt attention to the place of the cities in the practice of federalism; the cities assert their right to direct access to the federal government, while the states resist their demands. At issue is the fundamental question whether America shall continue to have a nominal two-way federalism, as it has had through most of our history; or whether the cities shall be given outright recognition, in practice if not in law, as operating partners in a three-way federalism. It is the thesis of this study that the trends point toward the emergence of a federal system that rests upon three partners rather than two. This chapter offers an analysis of the expanded partnership.

It should be emphasized that in at least three important senses the cities have long been active in the practice of federalism. The discussion in Chapter 2 of the quest for operational effectiveness

stressed the importance of the cities from early days as working partners in a cooperative federalism. Further, federal programs from the
beginning have recognized the significance of urban centers both for
the conduct of national activities and for the nation's economy. Post
offices and post roads, river and harbor improvements, and a wide
variety of governmental installations provide examples. So do the
activities of such agencies as the Departments of Commerce and
Labor, the Federal Bureau of Investigation, and the Federal Com-
munications Commission. None of these was established specifically
to serve the cities, but the program of each does in fact serve urban
needs in important ways. Further still, many of the federally in-
spired and supported programs that are administered by the states
have direct and significant impact on the cities. Among these are the
several public assistance programs and the federal-state highway
program. In 1963 the federal government contributed $5.7 billion—
almost 80 per cent of all federal grants-in-aid to the states—for
public assistance programs and highway building. That these programs have high importance for the cities, particularly in these later
days, goes almost without saying.

It remains true nevertheless that throughout much of our history the cities have not commanded special consideration *as cities*.
It has been only in recent decades that the municipalities have become sufficiently specialized to differentiate them in need from other
local governments. Again, throughout much of American history the
cities were not sufficiently large either to require or to command
special attention. As late as 1815 there were only seven incorporated
places in the country, while twenty-two of the fifty largest cities
were incorporated in 1850 or later. Until after 1900, a majority of
America's cities remained little more than rural trading and ship-
ping centers. There was no need and little demand to give such
places separate and special treatment. Still again, legal strait jackets
could be sundered more easily in the early days than now because
annexation was much more frequently employed to expand the
limits of the city. On the one hand, then, until some four decades
ago the cities were not sufficiently differentiated to require special
treatment, while on the other, such problems as arose could be ac-
commodated after a fashion under existing practice.

RISE OF FEDERAL-CITY RELATIONS

The covert and indirect recognition given to the cities as members of the federal system continued well into this century. Four forces were to conspire to modify the practice of American federalism, however, from about 1930 onward. First was the cash grant-in-aid which superseded the land-grant system after the substantial depletion of the public domain. The cash-grant system, though originating in the late years of the last century, came to full flower with the advent of President Franklin D. Roosevelt and the New Deal.[1] It has affected the latter-day practice of federalism as profoundly as any other single factor. Second was the depression of the 1930s, which spurred the launching of urgent and massive recovery programs to whose success the cities held the key. Third was the emergence following World War II of a metro-urban society attended by problems without precedent in their magnitude and complexity. Fourth was the demonstrated incapacity of the states to play an effective role in the war on urban problems.

In the circumstances it is not strange that the cities sought, and where opportunity offered embraced, new arrangements. Their recourse was to appeal direct to the federal government for assistance. The narrow and crooked paths of other years were broadened and straightened into expressways connecting the city halls and the national Capitol. Direct relations between Washington and the cities, long existent but as long submerged, were brought to the surface and recognized openly for what they were. The chief instrument by which this transformation was effected was the grant-in-aid.

The year 1932 constitutes a sort of geologic fault line in the development of the federal system. Prior to that year the American partnership nominally had been limited to the national government and the states; afterward the cities played an increasingly active and overt role in the practice of federalism. The most meaningful indicator of the growing urban prominence is the multiplying relations

[1] Brooke Graves reported that about two-thirds of all grant-in-aid programs in effect in 1958 rested upon legislation adopted since 1930. "Federal Grant-in-Aid Programs, 1803–1958" (Washington, D.C.: The Library of Congress, Legislative Reference Service, June 1958, processed), p. iv.

between the cities and the national government, and the most telling measure of those increasing relations is found in the growth of federal grants-in-aid direct to the cities. As late as 1932 such grants totaled no more than $10 million, virtually all of which went to the District of Columbia. Direct grant-in-aid relationships were, therefore, negligible in that year.

Table 4. Intergovernmental Payments for Selected Years, 1932–1963

(In millions of dollars)

Year	(1) Federal Payments to State and Local Governments	(2) Federal Payments to State Governments	(3) Federal Payments Direct to Local Governments	(4) State Payments to Local Governments
1963	8,507	7,566	941	10,906 (1962)
1960	6,974	6,382	592	9,443
1955	3,131	2,762	368	5,986
1950	2,486	2,275	211	4,217
1944	954	926	28	1,842
1940	945	667	278	1,654
1936	948	719	229	1,417
1932	232	222	10	801

Sources: 1932–1955, Columns 1, 2, and 3: U.S. Bureau of the Budget, "Historical Summary of Governmental Finances in the United States," 1957 Census of Governments, vol. IV, no. 3, 1959, Table 4.

1960, Columns 1, 2, and 3: U.S. Bureau of the Budget, *Governmental Finances in 1960,* September 19, 1961, Tables 1, 12.

1963, Columns 1, 2, and 3: U.S. Bureau of the Census, "Federal Payments to State and Local Governments, by Program: 1963" (processed tabulation compiled by the Governments Division).

Column 4: U.S. Bureau of the Census, Census of Governments: 1962, vol. VI, no. 2, *State Payments to Local Governments,* Table 1.

Table 4 affords a summary of the financial relations among governments for the three decades 1932–1963. Although the table warrants study at length, its message can be summarized in a few sentences. It will be evident at once that all categories of intergovernmental payments increased sharply from 1932 to 1963, most of them in steady progression. Federal payments to state and local governments increased almost 37 times during that period, federal payments to state governments somewhat more than 34 times, and state payments to local governments a little less than 14 times. The most significant figures for present purposes are contained in column 3; they reveal that federal payments direct to local governments multiplied more than 94 times in these three decades. It is worthy of emphasis that the growth rate of federal payments to local governments was almost three times that of federal payments to the states and almost seven times that of state payments to local governments.

The Governments Division of the Bureau of the Census for more than a decade has prepared an annual table showing "Federal Payments to State and Local Governments, by Program." The tabulation indicates that in 1963 federal payments to state and local governments totaled $8.5 billion. "Total Payments" included grants-in-aid, shared revenues, payments in lieu of taxes, payments for services, and a very small miscellaneous category. Grants-in-aid constituted 95 per cent of all payments. Not only did grants-in-aid dominate total payments to state and local governments in 1963, but they have also increased as a proportion of the total over the years: thus in 1953 grants comprised 89 per cent of the total, in 1958, 93 per cent. The tendency, therefore, in federal intergovernmental payments is toward great and increasing emphasis on the grant-in-aid. Our analysis here will emphasize the grant-in-aid.

Several general comments may be made about federal grant payments to state and local governments in 1963. The bulk of all such payments goes to the states; the 1963 figure was 88.4 per cent of the total. The localities therefore enjoy only limited assistance through direct federal grants. Public assistance and the federal-aid highway program accounted for almost 80 per cent of all grants-in-aid to the states. Also, of the amount paid direct to local governments, 5 per cent of the total went to the District of Columbia, which ordinarily is not considered a local government for the purposes of general analysis.

Federal grant-in-aid payments direct to local governments therefore are quite modest in amount; in 1963 the total figure came to little more than $893 million, or 11.6 per cent of all payments to state and local governments. But these direct payments, though not large, are nevertheless highly significant. In the first place, they are increasing: from 8 per cent of the total in 1958 to 11.6 per cent in 1963. From another viewpoint, federal grants to state and local governments increased 72 per cent from 1958 to 1963, while direct grants to local governments grew more than 248 per cent. In the second place, the programs for which federal grants were made direct to local governments (excepting those made exclusively to the District of Columbia) include the principal programs that have been devised to meet the new and urgent problems of the metro-city. Only six programs received grants of more than $25 million in 1963; these included watershed protection, airport development, low-rent public housing, slum clearance and urban renewal, the construction of waste treatment facilities, and assistance to schools in federally affected areas. All but the first are preponderantly urban in their impact. These programs received 88.4 per cent of all direct grants made. If to these six major programs are added two smaller but still significant ones—urban planning and public works–community facilities (each receiving in 1963 approximately $12 million)—the result is an expression in dollars of the federal government's concern (as of 1963) in the vast new urban problems that characterize metro-America.

The amounts involved are not large; total federal payments direct to local governments in 1963 were less than one-third of the amount granted to the states for highway building alone. But the purpose for which direct grants are made bestows upon them a significance much greater than the dollar amounts of the grants would suggest. Excepting the assistance to schools in federally affected areas, these grant programs are at the very eye of the urban hurricane. It was federal interest that encouraged the cities to launch them, and it is federal financial assistance that makes possible their continued existence. Many observers feel that the programs are far from adequate. Adequate or not, they symbolize the public commitment to this point in the war on the ills of urban America. And they rest squarely on federal concern and support.[2]

---

[2] There are other ways both to identify and to appraise federal-aid programs of interest to the cities. Thus the Advisory Commission on Intergovernmental Relations found that "By the end of 1962, the Federal Gov-

THREE JOINT PROGRAMS

How the cities and the national government work together in their direct relationships may best be discovered by examining selected joint programs in action. Three have been chosen for analysis here: the Federal-Aid Airport Program, the Slum Clearance and Urban Renewal Program, and the Low-Rent Public Housing Program. These three commanded almost half (48.6 per cent) of all direct grants-in-aid in 1963. Moreover, their proportion of the total is rising, though it fluctuates from year to year; in 1958 it was 42.6 per cent. These are long-range, well-established, widely accepted, and reasonably stable programs. They will provide a useful backdrop for an examination of federal-city relations in practice.

Federal-Aid Airport Program. The general purpose of the program authorized by the Federal Airport Act of 1946 is to bring about a national system of public airports adequate to meet the needs of civil aviation. To this end the federal government cooperates with the states and their subdivisions—municipalities, counties, special authorities—in the development of airports. The central feature of the program is federal assistance through grants-in-aid. Under the law the national government may contribute 50 per cent

---

ernment was administering more than 40 separate programs of financial aid for urban development, more than half of which were authorized after January 1950. Administration of these programs is distributed among many bureaus and divisions of five departments and eight independent agencies within the executive branch." Advisory Commission on Intergovernmental Relations, *Impact of Federal Urban Development Programs on Local Government Organization and Planning* (Washington, D.C.: Subcommittee on Intergovernmental Relations of the Committee on Government Operations, United States Senate, 89th Congress, 2d Session; Committee Print, 1964), p. 2. HHFA Administrator Robert C. Weaver (who is also a member of ACIR), in 1962 testimony before the above subcommittee, presented a seventeen-page list of "Federal Agency Programs Related to Urban Development" whose "total impact . . . [was] in the nature of $20 billion annually." (A mimeographed copy of the statement, dated December 14, 1962, was furnished by Dr. Weaver's office. The passage quoted appears on p. 2.) Any list that might be compiled for this study would be much more modest than either of these; for we emphasize only those programs which command federal support by direct grants in aid to the cities. Our purpose is not to evaluate the federal impact on urban governments but rather to assess the significance of the growing Washington-city relations for the federal system.

of the cost of developing an airport. (There are certain exceptions which need not concern us here.) The contribution may be applied either to the construction of a new airport or to the improvement of an old one, and may cover such items as land acquisition, site preparation, runway and taxiway paving, lighting and electrical work, utilities installations, roads (within airport boundaries only), removal of obstructions, and buildings.

The national organization for the administration of this program rests upon the Federal Aviation Act of 1958, which created a Federal Aviation Agency in succession to the Civil Aeronautics Administration.[3] The FAA has an Airports Service which reports directly to the Administrator and administers the Federal-Aid Airport Program. In view of the continuing relations of the Airports Service with literally hundreds of airports and aeronautic agencies throughout the country, its field organization is highly important. This consists of seven regional offices (located in New York City, Atlanta, Fort Worth, Kansas City, Los Angeles, Anchorage, and Honolulu), each under a regional director, and twenty-four district offices, each in charge of a district airport engineer.

In substance, the FAAP depends upon a national airport plan, which goes back to a requirement contained in the Federal Airport Act. The national plan is a permanent responsibility of the Airports Service, which is continually engaged in its revision.[4] The purpose of the plan is to spell out with care the locations and types of facilities deemed necessary, in the aggregate, to a national airport system. A revised version of the plan is published each year; it provides the framework within which decisions are made and actions taken for the ensuing grant period.

The first step toward consummation of a project agreement is taken by the prospective sponsor through submission of a request

[3] Public Law 85–726, 85th Congress; 72 Stat. 731.

[4] In the program's formative years there were some, including a number of governors, who argued that responsibility for developing a national airport plan should rest with the states. The decision in favor of a *national* plan was based upon a perceived need for an integrated plan and upon the conviction that the interest of the states in civil aviation was secondary. The considerations entering into the decision are summarized in *Legislative History of the Federal Airport Act* (Public Law 377, 79th Congress, Chapter 251, 2d Session), vol. One, *Senate Action* (April 1948), pp. 504–505.

for aid. Such a request contains information about the nature of the proposed project, its estimated cost, and the financial status of the sponsor. It is not binding on either party; on the contrary, it is regarded as nothing more than a declaration of interest and intent. At the same time, it does force the sponsor to give the project at least some advance thought, and it does give the federal authorities something to work toward. The request for aid often is drafted with the assistance of the (federal) district airport engineer.

With project requests in hand from all parts of the country, the Airports Service then proceeds to draw up an annual airport program for the agency's approval. Constructed within the framework provided by the national airport plan, the program comprises the projects established from the requests for aid received under the limits of the grant funds available This consideration necessitates ranking the proposed projects, which is done on the basis of their prospective contributions to the national system of airports.

Once the annual program is adopted, sponsors are notified of action taken and tentative allocations are set up for the projects included. Sponsors are then invited to submit detailed documents in support of each project, including a carefully drawn set of plans and specifications for all construction. Under a 1964 amendment to the law, the FAA may participate financially to the extent of 50 per cent of the cost in advance planning and engineering for airport layout plans and plans designed to lead to a project application. Following close scrutiny and approval of the project documents, a grant offer is made to the sponsor in behalf of the Federal Aviation Agency. Acceptance of the offer constitutes a contract between the sponsor and the federal government. Construction may then begin.[5]

The Federal-Aid Airport Program brings the sponsoring unit and the national government into close relation at many points. A large percentage of these contacts are informal and personal, in the sense that they develop naturally between FAA field men and local representatives. There are, however, many requirements designed to

[5] Federal Aviation Agency, *Federal-Aid Airport Program: Policies and Programming Standards* (September 1959). This booklet, prepared for the information of possible local sponsors, outlines with care the procedure summarized here.

encourage regularity in practice and ensure compliance with standards. The sponsor's request for federal aid, if it is to receive favorable consideration, must describe a project that fits into the national airport plan. The project request must win a place in the annual airport program, otherwise it cannot be approved for federal aid. The detailed project documents, submitted by the sponsor in response to the notice of tentative allocation of funds, must include plans and specifications meeting FAA standards for the development to be accomplished. There are certain regulations to which the sponsor must agree: construction contracts for more than $2,000 must be publicly advertised and must be awarded on the basis of competitive bids; minimum wage rates, determined by the Secretary of Labor, apply in the case of contracts for more than $2,000; employment preference must be given to veterans who have been honorably discharged; convict labor may not be employed; nondiscrimination in employment and in relations with labor must be ensured.

During construction, the project is subject to inspection by federal district engineers to the extent deemed necessary to ensure completion of the development contemplated. Each inspection evaluates the sponsor's supervision and construction control. It is followed by a technical report on progress, compliance with specifications, and adequacy of construction, which goes to the regional office for review. Final inspection is made by federal engineers when work is completed. All project cost records and accounts are subject to inspection by auditors, who are concerned with both the cost incurred and the service or item acquired. As in the case of engineering reports, the auditing reports go to the regional office, where the project cost is established.

Partial prepayments may be made against the federal grant as work progresses and inspection reports warrant. Conversely, prepayments may be withheld pending satisfaction of criticisms raised in unfavorable reports. Final federal payment is of course withheld until there is satisfactory proof of compliance with all contract terms. Determinations in all instances are made by the regional representatives under guides and standards set by the Washington office. New and difficult questions are submitted to Washington with the region's recommendation for a solution. Problems on which regional representatives disagree are sent to Washington for settlement. Washington officials review all matters handled by the region for the purposes of evaluating the effectiveness of policies and regional performance.

Throughout this discussion the term "sponsor" has been employed in referring to the local contracting party. The sponsor is almost always a municipality, although occasionally it is a county or other public agency. It will be recalled that the Federal Airport Act recognized the right of the states to participate in the airport program as actively as they might desire—a state may, for example, forbid its cities to deal directly with the FAA, and it may require all federal grant funds to be channeled through a state agency. It may be recalled further that the states fought for the privilege of serving as active partners in the FAAP, resisting vigorously the claim made by the cities to special recognition in the program. In view of the states' insistence on their "rights," it will be interesting to see how they have conducted themselves with respect to the program.

In 1961 it was reported that all states but two had aeronautics agencies. An imposing list of activities was attributed to these agencies, including planning and developing statewide systems of airports; expanding and improving scheduled air carrier service to communities; publishing maps, airport directories, and information bulletins; registering or licensing airports, pilots, and aircraft; enforcing safety regulations and air traffic rules; operating air search and rescue, disaster relief, and civil defense programs; conducting aviation safety and education programs; developing agricultural aviation; and erecting and painting aerial direction markers.[6] Only two years before, the same author reported that "state governmental plans and programs on aviation are still relatively unadvanced in some of the states. Approximately one-sixth of the states have no office, or even a single full-time official directly responsible for the promotion, development, and regulation of aviation within the

[6] A. B. McMullen, "Aviation among the States," in *The Book of the States, 1960–1961* (Chicago: Council of State Governments), pp. 332–336. Each biennial issue of *The Book of the States* carries a similar article by Col. McMullen, who is Executive Director of the National Association of State Aviation Officials.

state."[7] And four years later, thirty-three states were reported as having independent aeronautics departments or commissions, eleven as having aeronautics bureaus in another department (as commerce and public works)—a total of forty-four agencies reported in 1964 as against forty-eight claimed in 1961.[8]

It is fairly clear from the evidence at hand that some state aeronautics agencies are little more than paper organizations. The legal authorization is there, but often there is neither intent nor money to implement it. Although it was reported as early as 1957 that "Thirty states have adopted legislation requiring state approval of Federal-Aid Airport Program projects, and twenty-one states require FAAP funds to be channeled through their state aviation agencies,"[9] these requirements often were more honored in the breach than in the observance; and in any event, the legal requirements seldom were rigorously enforced. Regarding "channeling," some federal FAAP funds were in fact received by the state and paid to the sponsor on state certification and authorization; but frequently channeling was nothing more than a ritual. More than one airport director has testified that the state contributes nothing to the strength of the FAAP or to the soundness of its procedure, and that channeling through a state agency, where required and practiced, does nothing but add to paper work and delay.

Further evidence of the state's basic lack of interest in the airport program is found in the relevant financial reports for 1962. In that year only twelve states made payments of state funds to their cities for airport development. The amount contributed totaled $8,222,000.[10] In the same year FAAP funds paid direct to the localities (mostly municipalities) totaled $32,674,000.[11]

The data available indicate that the states did not take to airports in the years following 1946 as they took to highways after 1916. Two primary considerations suggest themselves by way of ex-

[7] *Ibid., 1958–1959,* p. 304.
[8] *Ibid., 1964–1965,* pp. 374–377.
[9] *Ibid., 1956–1957,* p. 292.
[10] U.S. Bureau of the Census, Census of Governments: 1962, vol. VI, no. 2, *State Payments to Local Governments,* pp. 19 ff.
[11] U.S. Bureau of the Census, Governments Division, "Federal Payments to State and Local Governments, by Program: 1962."

planation. One concerns the difference in magnitude between the highway and airport programs: the money spent on airports is minuscule by comparison with the billions of dollars poured into highways. The other concerns the programs themselves, which are quite different in nature. A highway is a statewide thing, quite at home as a rural thoroughfare. An airport, however, is a peculiarly urban facility which has little meaningful contact with the state outside the cities—and the larger cities at that. Here are two reasons— there are of course others—why the states have not risen to the challenge offered by those who equated airports with highways. Most states have been content to see the cities negotiate directly and contract with the United States government for funds under the Federal-Aid Airport Program, which therefore has developed as basically a federal-city undertaking.

In the seventeen years from 1947 to 1964 the federal government made grants for 5,817 developmental projects involving 1,888 airports in the fifty states, Puerto Rico, and the Virgin Islands. The total amount spent was somewhat more than $1,618,000,000, of which the federal government contributed about $795,350,000, or approximately 49 per cent.[12] There is no tabulation which shows the origins of the almost $823 million put into the program by project sponsors, though it is common knowledge that this was largely "local money." There has been some criticism of the program's limited scope and size, but little of its administration and almost none of the basic principle of federal-city cooperation on which, essentially, it rests.

Urban Renewal. Title I of the Housing Act of 1949 provided for a federal program of slum clearance and community development and redevelopment. This program, considered bold at the time, soon came to be regarded as too narrowly remedial in its approach; new slums formed faster than the old ones could be cleared away, and so the race was a losing one. The Housing Act of 1954 undertook to broaden the earlier measure by adopting the concept of preventive action through a more inclusive approach to the problems of

[12] Federal Aviation Agency, Airports Service, "1947–64 Federal-Aid Airport Program, Status as of June 30, 1964" (separate table).

blight and slums. Thus a positive note was injected into the slum clearance and urban redevelopment program, for which "urban renewal" was adopted as a more fitting title. Subsequent amendatory acts passed in 1956, 1959, and 1961 further expanded the urban renewal concept, notably in the direction of utilizing renewal for urban economic rehabilitation and tax-base revitalization and for improving job opportunities. Urban renewal, originally tied closely to housing, was viewed by these later statutes as having important contributions to make to the community's economic life as well. From 1954 forward, therefore, there has been a gradual shift toward increasing emphasis on the economic consequences of urban renewal, and an attendant growth in concern for the over-all effects of renewal activities on the community.[13]

The expanded urban renewal program seeks to prevent the spread of blight and to rescue and rehabilitate areas that can be restored to sound condition. It also continues the program of clearance and redevelopment of lost areas that was begun under the act of 1949. In the elaboration of these general objectives, the act as amended provides for federal financial assistance to the community of the nature and for the purposes indicated:

> *Advances* for the preparation of project plans. When the project goes into execution, the cost of planning becomes part of the overall cost of the project.
>
> *Temporary loans* which serve as the working capital for the project. The LPA is authorized to obtain temporary loans either directly from the Federal Government or, with the benefit of a Federal guarantee of payment, from private lending institutions. Because of the more favorable interest rates available, most loans are obtained by the latter method.
>
> *Capital grants* used to meet the Federal share of the net cost of the project.
>
> *Relocation grants* borne entirely by the Federal Government, to cover payments for the costs of moving and losses of property.
>
> *Definitive loans* made available to localities where land is disposed

[13] Urban Renewal Commissioner William L. Slayton discussed these trends in a *Statement before the Subcommittee on Housing, Committee on Banking and Currency, United States House of Representatives* (Washington, D.C.: Housing and Home Finance Agency, Urban Renewal Administration, November 21, 1963).

of under long-term leases rather than by sale. The loans may run for as long as 40 years and are repaid from the income under the lease.[14]

In all cases the recipient of federal assistance must be a local public body—municipality, county, special agency or authority—authorized by the state to engage in urban renewal activities. Normally the local entity is either a city or a local public agency (LPA) created to run the urban renewal program in close association with a city. In many cases one local public body deals with both public housing and urban renewal.

At the federal level the urban renewal program is directed by the Urban Renewal Administration, a unit within the Housing and Home Finance Agency. The continental United States is divided into six regions, with central offices in New York City, Philadelphia, Atlanta, Chicago, Fort Worth, and San Francisco. Each office is headed by a regional administrator, whose staff provides the principal point of both initial and continuing contact with the cities.

As a condition prerequisite to application for federal financial assistance, the local governing body (city council) must draw up a "workable program for community improvement." The workable program is, in effect, a plan in a very broad sense—it incorporates a detailed survey of the community's problems, together with a program for dealing with those problems. The elements of a workable program include an adequate set of codes and ordinances, a comprehensive community plan, neighborhood analyses ("an extension of the planning process to each neighborhood"), an administrative organization judged to be effective in terms of program requirements, a program for relocating displaced families, demonstration of financial soundness, and provision for active citizen participation.[15] The HHFA Administrator must approve its workable program before a city may proceed further. Certified originally for one year, the

[14] *Ibid.,* p. 398. In normal circumstances the federal government's capital grant covers two-thirds of the net project cost. The locality contributes the remaining third.

[15] Housing and Home Finance Agency, "The Workable Program for Community Development: Fact Sheet" (Washington, D.C.: Housing and Home Finance Agency, Office of the Administrator, March 1964).

program must be recertified annually if the community is to remain eligible to receive federal aid under activities that require it.[16]

The process by which an urban renewal project comes into being may be outlined briefly as follows:

1. The city council creates a local public renewal agency, which thereupon assumes responsibility for carrying forward the renewal process. Its major initial responsibility is to prepare and present an application for federal survey and planning assistance.

2. On receipt of notice of URA approval of its survey and planning application, the LPA proceeds with the planning of its project. At this point the community may seek a planning advance. URA policy limits the planning period to eighteen months, though it may be extended for cause.

3. The urban renewal plan, when completed, is submitted to the URA for approval.

4. By federal law the local governing body (city council) must approve the plan in its final form. In conjunction with the approval process, a local public hearing must be held. Local law may require other approvals, as for example by the city planning agency.

5. If on examination the procedural requirements are found to have been met, the URA draws up a loan and grant contract, which on approval becomes binding on the signatory parties.

6. The local public agency is now authorized to begin work on the project; in technical terms, the project is now in the loan-and-grant stage.[17]

To this point all steps taken have been in a sense preliminary. The substance of urban renewal manifests itself in the project execution stage, whose major phases are:

1. Land acquisition. The local public agency proceeds to acquire the property covered by the project, through either negotiated purchase or condemnation.

[16] The workable program concept is not limited to urban renewal, but extends to other HHFA programs as well.

[17] David L. Lutin, "The Current Federally Aided Urban Renewal Program: What It Is and How It Works" (New York: Committee for Economic Development, mimeographed, n.d.). This paper affords a succinct summary of these procedures at pp. 14–16. See also Commissioner Slayton's statement, *op. cit.,* pp. 441–442.

2. Relocation. The occupants to be displaced, individuals, families, and businesses, must be relocated and rehoused in order to make the property available for the next phase.

3. Site clearance and preparation. This involves demolition of buildings on land to be cleared, along with steps for the rehabilitation and conservation of properties to be saved.

4. Land disposal. Once the land is cleared, proposals for disposal must be worked out, values determined, redeveloper(s) selected, and sales effectuated. A project is declared completed when all land has been disposed of.

In addition to these major stages, there are ancillary steps to be taken along the way. The property acquired, for example, must be managed from acquisition to final disposition. The negotiations surrounding a sizable project are exceedingly complex, involving as they do local property owners and occupants, potential redevelopers, and governments at every level (the local governing body, on occasion the state, and sometimes several federal agencies). Active throughout the process is the Urban Renewal Administration, which reviews and approves or concurs in each important step, inspects for compliance with standards, and conducts an audit and certifies the final grant requisition. On the ground the project is in the hands of the local public agency, which, subject to state law and to whatever jurisdiction is retained by the city council, exercises considerable authority.[18]

A number of generalizations about urban renewal procedure may be offered. Although the process outlined above appears to be quite complicated, it should be remembered that the community benefits from the technical assistance of professional urban renewal staff members from the workable program to the completed contract. The regional office furnishes the bulk of this assistance, which,

[18] Commissioner Slayton, *op. cit.*, outlines the execution stage with care at pp. 443–445. The Public Housing Administration and the Federal Housing Administration are available to assist in relocating displaced families, the former by providing low-rent housing, the latter by insuring mortgages for the construction of low-cost private housing. It is worthy of mention that Section 220 of the National Housing Act authorizes mortgage insurance in an urban renewal context under terms more favorable than FHA usually is able to offer.

it must be said, is kept to a modest level by limited resources. The law also provides for federal financial aid to the community, in the form of advances or loans, at every important stage in the process. It will not be forgotten that urban renewal is a nationwide program and that the federal government is committed to bearing a large share of its costs. The national government exerts considerable influence over the whole process, not through the positive power of coercion but through the potential sanction of withholding assistance. The nature of federal influence nevertheless is such as to leave a large measure of autonomy with the communities. Last, apart from the procedural requirements, the inescapable physical problems involved ensure that urban renewal will be a slow-moving program.

As of June 1, 1964, there were 1,454 urban renewal projects on the books. Of these, 40.5 per cent were in the planning stage, 50 per cent were in execution, and 9.5 per cent (138 projects) had been completed. These represented commitments totaling somewhat more than $3.9 billion (out of a total of $4 billion authorized). In addition to urban renewal projects as such, the URA was or had been involved in 219 general neighborhood renewal plans, 115 community renewal programs, 55 feasibility surveys, and 49 demonstration grant contracts. It will be some years before the full effects of the program will be felt; the projects completed thus far are both comparatively few and for the most part relatively small and unimposing (the 9.5 per cent of all projects that have been completed used only 2.4 per cent of the money committed.) [19] Immediate improvement in physical appearance can already be observed in many communities; but the program's long-range, cumulative effect on the economy and the way of life of the cities remains for future realization.

One thing is clear: urban renewal is essentially a big-city program, for the conditions the program seeks to alleviate are particularly severe in the large cities. All cities of more than one million

[19] "Report of Urban Renewal Operations, May 1964" (Washington, D.C.: Housing and Home Finance Agency, Urban Renewal Administration), pp. 2–3. The "projects completed" criterion provides only a crude index of achievement, partly because projects often are "held open" (that is, are considered to be not completed) for technical reasons after work on them is finished.

population have urban renewal projects, as do 86 per cent of all cities over 250,000. Only 65 per cent of the cities over 50,000 have gone into urban renewal, and the figure drops to 53.3 per cent for the cities over 25,000 population.[20] The smaller cities are not strangers to the problem of internal deterioration, but the urban renewal program nevertheless has offered greater hope to the larger cities. It is in truth aimed directly at one of the core problems of metropolitan America.

The states generally have not manifested any enthusiasm for, or even any special interest in, urban renewal. As many as forty-five states have provided the enabling legislation to make possible local participation. This is, of course, minimal recognition of the program, but in most states it is also maximal. From year to year as many as three or four states may make contributions (or loans) in partial support of urban renewal activities. One such state is New York, which since 1961 has made loans to its communities in the amount of one-half of the local contributions required to match federal urban renewal grants. In 1962 New York's payments to its cities for urban renewal *and* housing amounted to $20.4 million; only one other state, Massachusetts, reported a similar payment, and it was quite modest by comparison.[21] The same year witnessed a federal contribution of $160 million direct to the cities for slum clearance and urban renewal. At the 1961 meeting of the American Institute of Planners, Governor Gaylord Nelson of Wisconsin summarized the situation in these words:

> Most of our states have been content to allow the federal government to direct unilaterally the huge task of urban renewal. If we continue to abdicate to the federal government in this area, the states will

[20] *Urban Renewal Project Characteristics, December 31, 1963* (Washington, D.C.: Housing and Home Finance Agency, Urban Renewal Administration), p. 7. Another set of figures can be developed to show that urban renewal is quite popular among the smaller cities. Thus at the end of 1962 it could be reported that 20 per cent of the cities participating in the program had less than 10,000 people (Housing and Home Finance Agency, *16th Annual Report*, p. 280). Such data do not negate the conclusion that urban renewal devotes the bulk of its resources to and makes its greatest impact on the major cities.

[21] U.S. Bureau of the Census, Census of Governments: 1962, vol. VI, no. 2, *State Payments to Local Governments*, pp. 19 ff.

have lost the opportunity to respond to one of the great challenges of our time—the battle against slums, obsolescence, and flight from the city.[22]

The inescapable fact is that urban renewal, preoccupied as it is with urban problems, is in a very special sense a metro-municipal concern. The state neither senses an urgent moral involvement nor acknowledges a financial obligation with respect to this activity.

Low-Rent Public Housing. Like federal aid in airport development, low-rent public housing originated in response to depression needs. Thus the National Industrial Recovery Act (PL 67, 73d Congress) provided for participation by the national government in "low-cost housing and slum clearance projects" as early as 1933. The Emergency Relief Appropriation Act (PL 11, 74th Congress), passed in 1935, provided $450 million for housing. By 1937, as many as fifty low-rent public projects had been approved under these early acts.

Most historians of housing, noting that early legislation emphasized public works rather than housing as such, point to the United States Housing Act of 1937 (PL 412, 75th Congress) as the first major measure to deal directly with low-rent public housing. The act undertook:

> To provide financial assistance to the States and political subdivisions thereof for the elimination of unsafe and insanitary housing conditions, for the eradication of slums, for the provision of decent, safe, and sanitary dwellings for families of low income, and for the reduction of unemployment and the stimulation of business activity, [and] to create a United States Housing Authority. . . .[23]

A number of amendatory acts have been passed since 1937. Chief among these is the Housing Act of 1949 (PL 171, 80th Congress), which signaled the beginning of a much-expanded public housing program; and those of 1956 (PL 1020, 84th Congress), 1961 (PL 70, 87th Congress), and 1964 (PL 560, 88th Congress).

The Housing Act of 1937, as amended, provides for a nation-

[22] Quoted in *The Book of the States, 1962–1963,* p. 456.
[23] "The United States Housing Act of 1937, as Amended" (Washington, D.C.: Housing and Home Finance Agency, Public Housing Authority, September 23, 1959).

wide program of low-rent public housing. Housing projects are built, owned, and managed by local housing authorities, which in turn are created by the designated local governments under authority granted by state enabling legislation. The law further provides that the federal government shall make available to the local housing authorities both technical assistance and financial aid, in the manner presently to be indicated. Low-rent housing is designed to serve the needs of those of low income who otherwise would not be able to afford "decent, safe, and sanitary dwellings." Clientele given special consideration are low-income veterans (and their survivors), Indians, and the elderly. Public housing likewise is designed to serve an important slum-clearance function, and in that connection to work closely with the urban renewal and redevelopment program.

The process by which a public housing project comes into being may be outlined briefly:

1. A local government creates a local housing authority (LHA) and the two enter into an agreement of cooperation in respect to the forthcoming housing development. The major considerations covered by this agreement are: The local government undertakes to provide the standard municipal services for the project; and the LHA agrees to make payments in lieu of taxes to the local government in an amount not to exceed 10 per cent of the shelter rentals produced by the project. (Implicit in this statement is the fact that the federal housing law specifically exempts housing projects from taxation.)

2. The LHA then approaches the Public Housing Administration (through a regional representative) with a proposal for construction of a given number of public housing units. If a preliminary survey discloses the proposal to be in order, the PHA makes a "reservation" in behalf of the program. This means simply that the PHA is prepared to assist in carrying the program forward in the event the legal requirements are satisfactorily met.

3. The LHA executes a preliminary loan contract with the PHA by which funds are provided for the initial planning of the project: site selection, architectural sketches, market surveys, and so on.

4. The LHA submits a workable program, which comprises a

comprehensive blueprint for community development and which must be approved by the Housing and Home Finance Administrator.

5. When plans have developed, the LHA and the PHA enter into an annual contributions contract. This covers both a PHA loan to finance the project's development cost and continuing annual contributions to enable the LHA to maintain the low-rent status of the project. It also covers the conditions and the terms under which the LHA will develop and manage the project.

6. As the project approaches completion, arrangements are made for its long-term financing: the LHA sells bonds (normally forty-year serial bonds) to cover site and construction costs, and to repay all PHA loans.

7. Finally, the project, completed, enters the management stage. Qualifications for occupancy are established, rents fixed, units rented, project income computed, and the net annual deficit (to be covered by annual contributions from PHA) determined. The project is now said to be "under management."

Throughout this process the Public Housing Administration plays an active and positive role. The PHA, a constituent agency of the Housing and Home Finance Agency, operates through regional offices which for the continental United States number six. The organization of a regional office indicates the nature of PHA's concerns. Each office typically has an assistant director for development, another for management. The assistant director for development usually administers sections having to do with project planning, land acquisition, construction, and technical services. The assistant director for management presides over sections whose functions relate to management review, occupancy, operations engineering, and fiscal managment. These descriptive terms suggest what is in fact the case, that the PHA (through its regional office) is vitally interested in every step from preliminary planning to management operations.

Its interest, as intimated earlier, takes the form in part of technical assistance in preparing application and other required papers, assembling land for the site, making arrangements for planners and architects, soliciting and evaluating bids, inspecting during construction, preparing occupancy standards, fixing rents, preparing operating budgets, and computing the spread between income and bond amortization requirements (on the basis of which annual contributions by PHA will be calculated). Finally, in the management phase PHA continues its technical assistance for a host of operating problems concerning which the national agency has had much experience, the LHA in many cases little or none. The technical assistance rendered by PHA's regional representatives is critical, for it brings federal experience and expertise to bear on technical problems largely beyond the ken of the typical local housing authority. Federal loans and grants likewise are critical, for in their absence there would be no national public housing program.

As of July 31, 1964, the Low-Rent Public Housing Program embraced 4,805 projects comprising 710,145 dwelling units. Of the more than 4,800 projects, 73.6 per cent were in managemnt, 7.0 per cent were under construction, and 19.4 per cent were in the preconstruction stage. The occupancy rate (March 31, 1964) was 98.4 per cent. The "average" occupant family (1962) had four members, earned $2,460 yearly, and paid a monthly rental of $43. At the end of 1962, twenty-five years after the passage of the first major housing act, more than two million people lived in public housing dwellings.[24]

Certain features of the housing program are worthy of emphasis. First, ownership of all public housing projects resides with the local housing authorities, which also bear the responsibility for their management. Second, neither state nor locality makes any financial contribution toward the construction or operation of any project. Local governments do make substantial contributions in service, but they are compensated, in part at least, through LHA payments in lieu of taxes. Third, the federal government maintains close and continuing contact with any particular housing project from the earliest planning stage forward. Fourth, public housing, like both the airport and the urban renewal programs, places major emphasis on the larger cities. At the end of 1962 there were 1,371 local housing authorities in the United States (including Puerto Rico and the

[24] The Statistics Branch, Program Planning Division, Public Housing Administration publishes a steady stream of statistics both on the physical aspects of public housing and on the social and economic characteristics of its occupants. These data were taken from miscellaneous short publications and releases obtainable from PHA's information office on a current basis.

Virgin Islands). Of the programs sponsored by these authorities, two-thirds were outside urbanized areas in places of 25,000 population or less. The figure is deceptive, however, because, when all is said and done, only a minor percentage of the smaller places have public housing programs, and the projects located in the smaller places do not loom large in the total public housing picture. At the other extreme, all cities of one million or more have such programs, as do 87 per cent of those between 250,000 and one million in population.[25] Although low-rent public housing is not exclusively a big-city program, it does nonetheless serve the needs primarily of the larger cities. A deficiency in housing is, after all, one of the major characteristics of the twentieth-century metro-society.

Fifth, whereas airport development and urban renewal are preponderantly federal-local programs, public housing is exclusively so. The states are neither required nor expected to make financial contributions to the program, and they make none. All states save four (Iowa, Oklahoma, Utah, and Wyoming) have passed enabling statutes permitting local governments to set up local housing authorities, and that is the extent of state participaion in the federal-local Low-Rent Public Housing Program. It should be recorded that a few states—notably New York, Pennsylvania, and Massachusetts—have their own public housing programs. These, however, have no relation with the program of the Public Housing Administration, hence need not concern us here.

SOME OBSERVATIONS
ON THE EXPANDED PARTNERSHIP

Other examples of the expanded partnership—the waste treatment facilities, open space, and mass transit programs, to illustrate—might be cited, but in general they would merely reconfirm the story sketched in outline for the airport development, urban renewal, and public housing programs. It is not difficult to identify the main drift of the story or, at least in a general way, to assess its significance. The account clearly signalizes the emergence of the cities as public partners in the American federal system. They have been silent

[25] Housing and Home Finance Agency, *16th Annual Report* (Washington, D.C., 1962), p. 205.

partners for decades through the practice of cooperative federalism, as we have noted. The difference since 1932 is that the cities now are accepted openly as members of the federal family; they now do overtly, continuously, and as a matter of course what they used to do quietly, sporadically, and with some lingering doubt as to propriety. The channels between the cities and the federal government have become broader, deeper, and more direct since 1932 than they were before.

The principal vehicle for the accomplishment of this peaceful revolution has been, as we have seen, the cash grant-in-aid. In briefest terms and in the present context, this is a device by which a program of both urban and national significance is undertaken by the cities with the technical assistance and financial support of the national government. The grant-in-aid has outrun other forms of state and local revenue of late years; a recent publication disclosed that intergovernmental revenue (payments to state and local governments by the federal government) had increased faster than any other source of state and local revenue during the decade 1952–1962.[26] Reference to Table 4 (page 112) will serve to remind that payments by the federal government direct to local governments have increased much more rapidly than any other form of intergovernmental payment.

The role of local government is not to be minimized in these new and growing federal-local programs. There must be a local public agency, whether the local governing body itself or a quasi-independent agency named by it, to assume responsibility as the local sponsoring (planning-constructing-operating) authority. In the beginning there was no manifest federal interest in or concern for the organization of local government; the federal agency (FAA, URA, PHA) was of necessity program oriented, and it took action to further its program without much reference to the impact of its policies on local government. Recently, some evidence of a softening in this hard programmatic line has been discerned.

But if each program relies upon local project sponsorship, each also emphasizes federal responsibility. In the three programs ex-

[26] Advisory Commission on Intergovernmental Relations, *Tax Overlapping in the United States,* 1964 (Washington, D.C.: ACIR, July 1964), p. 5.

amined, the federal regional representatives were never very far away. They were found to be ever ready to assist with planning, economic, engineering, and management counsel and aid. The national government in truth has a major stake in a given grant-in-aid program, and each federal agency has developed procedures for effectively asserting and safeguarding the federal interest. These include, in addition to the devices for technical assistance, specifications regarding plans, standards, and records, the requirement of both occasional and periodic reports, review of procedures at strategic points, and inspection to check compliance with specifications.

It is worthy of emphasis that there is no initial compulsion in any federal-local program. The original decision regarding local participation in a program lies with the state, and some states have refused to pass the necessary enabling legislation. The locality always retains the option of refusing to participate, and many communities have exercised that option with respect to one program or another. There is, of course, compulsion on the local sponsor to comply with federal standards once agreement has been reached to take part in a program. The basic decision whether or not to participate is, however, a matter for state and local determination.

As the federal agencies gain in maturity, they manifest an increasing inclination toward a broader (that is, a less narrowly programmatic) view. Illustrations are found in the growing emphasis on local comprehensive planning and in the beginnings of cooperation among the agencies in Washington. This is not the place to examine this point in detail. It is sufficient to note the beginnings of a trend toward a broader and more general view of government, and particularly of federal-local relations, among the agencies in Washington.

In final comment, it may be observed that the role to be played by the states vis-à-vis two of the three federal-local programs examined—and a number of others as well—is a matter for state determination. With regard to the airport development and the urban renewal programs, the states may participate as actively as they please; for the federal legislation is quite permissive with respect to state action. That the states generally have not chosen to take an active part in these programs is a comment both upon state orientation and upon the problems to which the programs are addressed. Essentially these are matters for urban, and more particularly metropolitan, rather than state concern. As we noted earlier, the problems are discontinuous, and they symbolize the metropolitan-industrial society of the future rather than the rural-agrarian society of America's past. Inasmuch as many states seem more concerned with where America has been than with where it is going, the decision not to become too heavily involved in urban matters is a natural one. And given the predilections of the state, it may also be a wise one.

6.

Three Views of the Expanded Partnership

How the expanded partnership looks will depend upon the position from which it is regarded; that is, on the point of view of the observer. Three observers whose views are relevant are the partners in the broadened federal system. Each has its own value system against which to weigh the federal-city programs, each has its own set of purposes and goals to be served, and each experiences problems that differ in nature and severity with varying history, status, and outlook. Let us see how the new federalism looks from Washington, from the community, and from the state capital respectively.

WASHINGTON: THE VIEW FROM ABOVE

"Washington" as used here means the federal government, or more accurately the spokesmen for and representatives of that government, whether situated in the national capital or in some one of the numerous regional and district offices. Washington's official involvement in federal-city relations is limited to the few major programs from which most of those relations spring. Washington's interest is, therefore, programmatic. It is also pragmatic, and not much (not at all legally) concerned with the broader question of federal-city relations and the federal system.

Federal officials are interested in community organization and performance primarily for two reasons. First, the statutes whose

137

programs they administer set forth certain goals along with standards and procedures for achieving them. Second, the national treasury provides large sums of money to the communities for these programs: in 1963, more than $36 million for airports, almost $164 million for public housing, over $183 million for urban renewal, and $51 million for waste treatment facilities, to mention the four largest. These sums would not buy many space craft, but they are nevertheless sufficiently large to warrant an active interest in the way they are handled. The federal government's concern for the community rests, therefore, upon considerations of policy and cost.

Federal means of influencing community practice in the interest of achieving desired policy and cost standards are several. They vary in detail from program to program though in purpose, and generally in method as well, they are fairly uniform. For purposes of illustration, let us examine the procedures of the Urban Renewal Administration. There are nine principal methods of control to ensure community compliance with program standards.

The first is the "workable program for community improvement," which as we have observed is a device for compelling (and assisting) the community to take a long, careful look at its current situation, its goals, and its resources. The workable program must be certified by the Housing and Home Finance Administrator before the community may make application for federal assistance; moreover, it must be recertified each year. The workable program requirement first brings federal and local representatives into substantial contact.

Second, each community must submit a formal application for the assistance desired. The application is reviewed with care by federal officials to determine both conformance with statutory objectives and the capacity of the community to support the undertaking in question.

Third, the locality prepares and federal representatives review a budget to control the expenditure of the grant funds to be made available for the project. Inasmuch as all cost elements—salaries, office rentals, travel costs, and so on—are included, the budget offers a far-reaching means of control.

Fourth, approval of the application for assistance is followed by a contract between the local agency and the federal government. The contract covers such important items as work to be undertaken, policies and procedures to be employed, standards to be met, and work schedule to be observed. The contract follows a form fixed by the federal government, and it commits the community to execution of the program in line with the policies and standards set.

Fifth, federal policies and procedures are set out in great detail in the manual of policies and requirements, and from time to time in other policy statements as well. New federal employees are required as an early assignment to become thoroughly familiar with the manual, and local representatives are urgently invited to familiarize themselves with it. The manual is perhaps the most important single means of procuring compliance with policy.

Sixth, field inspections provide a most important means of performance control. Such inspections are performed throughout the life of a project by representatives from the regional office. In substantive terms they serve as the most effective means of ensuring that the project is carried out in accordance with requirements. The inspector's chief reliance is the manual.

Seventh, the local authority is required to submit a variety of reports regarding both financial and physical operations throughout the life of a project. Such reports are regarded as primarily informational in nature; nevertheless they often provide data on which to base measures to correct ineffective local practice.

Eighth, some steps taken by the local authority are so important that prior federal approval is required. This is true, for example, of the process of land acquisition, which federal representatives follow very closely. It is true also of local advertisements for private loans to finance project activities.

Finally, the program agencies conduct annual audits of every project. In addition, they make other spot audits (or reviews) of a technical character. The General Accounting Office makes occasional audits of selected projects. The audit has limited use as a method of positive control, but the prospect of an audit serves to keep the local authority alert, and in particular more attentive to detail.

These devices provide the federal government with a variety of means for persuading the community to observe policy standards and cost limitations. These methods prevail throughout the country. Theoretically they are employed without variation wherever federal-city projects are found. Realistically, however, the use of this arsenal differs from place to place and project to project as conditions vary and situations require. It follows therefore that the position of the community in the expanded federal-city system is determined not by rule alone but by a combination of rule and circumstance. A number of nonlegal factors, in addition to the perceived legal ones, intervene to give the federal-city system flexibility and so to make it workable in real-life situations.

Certain factors that profoundly affect federal-city relations stem from the statutes themselves. With respect to the public housing program, there is no local cash participation. The federal government contributes not some predetermined amount but the full cost of the project. Moreover, the federal government's commitment to a particular public housing project runs for forty years, during which time any excess of operating receipts over operating costs is applied to reduction of the federal subsidy. The result of this method of financing—which has often been called an ingenious one—is to intensify federal watchfulness in an effort to protect the national investment, as well as to relieve the local housing agency of both interest in and responsibility for conducting an economical operation. Regarding urban renewal, the federal government obligates itself to pay two-thirds of the gross cost of a particular project. Such costs are not known until the project is completed. "Project costs" require both careful initial definition and continued surveillance. So does the concept of noncash grants, which encourages the community to charge as much of its public works program as possible to its urban renewal program as part of its one-third of the gross project costs. Urban renewal therefore also requires (or in the past was judged to require) close supervision in the interest of protecting federal investments.

Some federal spokesmen also see the autonomous local agencies employed in the administration of the public housing and urban renewal programs as another factor requiring close federal supervision. The cities, the argument goes, over the years have built up strong budget, personnel, procurement, auditing, and accounting systems, so that they are now among the best-managed of all American governments. Not so the local housing authorities and the local public agencies, which have little management competence save that gained through their federal connections. Nor are the cities much concerned with these autonomous agencies (there are notable exceptions), because they have no responsibility for them. If the cities were themselves responsible for the urban renewal and public housing programs, the federal agencies could relax their surveillance, for the programs would then be in competent, experienced, and proven hands. Under the system of administration by independent authorities, the federal agencies feel they have no option to the exercise of fairly firm central control. Nevertheless the trend is toward reduced federal supervision, thanks to constant improvement in local management and to pressure on Congress for greater local autonomy.

A major nonlegal factor affecting federal-city relations is the attitude of the national administration toward a particular program. The Eisenhower administration looked with disfavor on some federal-city undertakings; in a broader sense, indeed, it frowned on the principle of grants in aid and sought to "return" to the states both certain programs and certain revenue sources for their support. Given this background it is not surprising that some federal-city grant-in-aid programs went into doldrums. Local leaders became convinced that it was the unannounced purpose of some high federal officials to scuttle their programs. This atmosphere fostered a spirit of mutual distrust and suspicion: the professional associations of local administrators lost touch with the federal executives, who in their turn came to regard the organizations as biased and self-centered. But if the environment was not generally favorable from 1952 to 1960, a remarkable change occurred in the latter year. Federal-local relations since 1960 have thrived as never before, due very largely to a drastic change in "front office" attitude.

Another important consideration which shapes federal-city relations inheres in the age and outlook of the federal agency. Many observers compare public housing and urban renewal to the disadvantage of the former. Public housing, they say, is a stable, mature program with nothing exciting in prospect. Its administrators have grown old with the program. They have lost their youthful zest, and have become a host of maintenance men wedded to routine procedures. The Public Housing Administration, it is said, is more interested in maintaining the *status quo* than in searching out new ways to adapt its program to public needs. In contrast, the same observers say, is the Urban Renewal Administration, which has not yet settled down to a firm and predictable routine. It is led by young and energetic executives, and its personnel includes a sizable percentage of recent university graduates. As a youthful, vigorous agency, the URA is searching for ways to adapt its program to the growing needs of the cities. Its representatives approach their tasks in a positive, what-can-we-do-for-you frame of mind. The differences in spirit, attitude, and point of view between the public housing and the urban renewal agencies seem unmistakable, particularly to the local executives and commissioners who deal with both. They agree that the Public Housing Commissioner since 1960 has made a vigorous effort to close the gap between the two, but they also maintain that the PHA has certain characteristics, as a result of age and maturity, which make it very difficult to energize.

A final conditioning factor affecting federal-city relations concerns the attitude of the agency and its chief administrative officers toward the manual of policies and regulations. Again many observers cite the Public Housing and the Urban Renewal Administrations for illustration. PHA officials, they maintain, regard the manual as inviolable. "It's in the book" is regarded as sufficient justification for any directive, "It's not in the book" as adequate reason to deny any request. Urban renewal representatives, on the other hand, consider the manual to be advisory or permissive rather than conclusive. They search for ways of expediting program action, and so will approve any reasonable proposal that is not directly contrary to manual requirements. In the one case the manual is employed to obstruct action, in the other to expedite it. Critics of the PHA agree that there has been an effort since 1960 to give a more positive interpretation to the housing manual; still, they maintain, the advantage lies with the URA when the manual procedures and requirements of the two agencies are compared.

In part the difference in attitude regarding the manual and its uses grows from a basic difference in perceived relations between the federal government and the cities. Adverting to the statutory requirements examined earlier, the PHA feels a responsibility for fairly close supervision over the local housing authorities for a period of forty years; whereas the URA holds that supervision need not be so close, and certainly the period of surveillance is not so long. Involved also is the issue of close federal supervision versus local autonomy, and this cannot be resolved in terms of logic or doctrine alone. All national agencies of any considerable experience are acquainted with cities that have earned the right to a large measure of autonomy, as well as other cities that require close and continued supervision for the protection of federal interests. In an important sense, then, the manner in which manual rules are to be interpreted and applied must be "played by ear." It should be noted that in recent years there have been positive efforts on the part of all federal agencies to condense and simplify their manual requirements, and that even the most outspoken critics of federal supervision are both conscious and appreciative of these efforts.

The problems confronting the federal agencies in regard to federal-city relations may be divided into two major classes. The first concerns the matter of interagency (or interprogram) relations. Not less than half a dozen Washington agencies have major program responsibilities, and there has been little effort to correlate federal activities in the past. The problem is one of coordination of efforts, or even of administrative reorganization to admit of more effective program planning. A second aspect of the problem of coordination is found in the community, where each federally-aided program goes its separate way without much (certainly without adequate) attention to others which may be related, and where the programs emphasize the localities individually without regard for the proliferation of local units. Regarding the first problem it is clear that coordination at the consumer level is difficult without prior coordination in Washington. As to the second, the difficulties stem from what we have called the metropolitan problem. It will receive attention in the next chapter.

Concerning federal-city relations as such, three aspects of the same major problem emerge. The first involves confining relations to proper channels. Federal representatives sometimes overstep the bounds of propriety in the matter of relations, although the offender usually is a local person. Mayors in particular find it difficult to "go up the line" step by step. They are accustomed to direct and above all to political action, and many of them see no resaon why they should not deal at once with the agency chiefs in Washington. Those chiefs often refer such an inquiry or request back to the regional director, but sometimes the circumstances are such that they are compelled to take immediate action. This is particularly true when local contact is made directly with a member of Congress, who then calls an agency chief in behalf of his constituent. Such occurrences are by no means uncommon. They fly in the face of approved practice, and cause all manner of intra-agency strains. They result in a great deal of embarrassment and no small number of serious problems for the administrators.

Another aspect of the problem stems from local pressures on federal representatives. These arise in part from the mistaken assumption by citizens both that the federal government is solely responsible for a particular federal-city program and that federal representatives are in a position to deal with citizen complaints. Federal officials spend an appreciable part of their time referring citizen inquiries (suggestions, requests, complaints) to the proper local authority. A different pressure is exerted by the local official who desires the federal agency to assume responsibility for some new or difficult problem—the noise made by jet airplanes, for example. Any severe problem that raises new and untested issues is likely to be "bucked up" to the federal government, whose administrators must be constantly alert lest they overstep acceptable program bounds. In this connection the testimony of a local program director is apposite. "We wouldn't do away with federal supervisors if we could," he affirmed. "We need somebody we can appeal to, somebody who can say 'No' more forcefully than we can."

Finally there is the problem of maintaining federal surveillance of local authorities at a proper level of intensity. There are both centralizers and local autonomists at all levels in the federal hierarchy. There are also local authorities who want, indeed who need, more technical assistance, as well as those who would be done with all federal connections—except, of course, for the grant. Federal administrators, highly conscious of these conflicting views, are keenly aware of their responsibilities under the grant-in-aid system. Federal officials, as we have observed, are concerned with both local policy direction and fiscal regularity in regard to local grant-in-aid programs. The establishment and operation of a system of surveillance that will allow maximum local autonomy while ensuring effective discharge of this responsibility is a core problem of federal-city relations. It commands the constant attention of high federal executives concerned with the administration of the expanded partnership.

THE COMMUNITY: THE VIEW FROM BELOW

Most individuals engaged in the practice of local government are neither philosophers nor, in any broad sense, students of government. This is true of those who run the affairs of the cities, which are by consensus the best-managed of the units of general local government. The mayors and council members know the city and its people, their wants, their needs, their resources, their problems; and the program administrators are well acquainted with their agencies and the activities they pursue, and with agency relations with the city and with organizations involved in kindred activities. It is no criticism of urban officials to note that few have had the time or occasion to examine federal-city relations in theoretical or conceptual terms. Interviews with something like a hundred of these officials—mayors, councilmen, urban renewal and public housing administrators, airport directors, and members of citizen commissions—indicate both that they are well versed in the problems arising from operational relations and that they have definite ideas about how these problems might be resolved. This section explores the community's view of the expanded partnership, as recorded by those most intimately involved in it.[1]

[1] Two recent public reports treat of this subject. The first, *Views on Public Housing* (Washington, D.C.: Housing and Home Finance Agency, March 1960), comprises a symposium of letters written in response to a request by Norman P. Mason, then HHFA Administrator. The second, *The Federal System as seen by State and Local Officials* (Washington, D.C., 1963) summarizes the results of a questionnaire dealing with intergovern-

There is wide agreement among community spokesmen regarding a number of important points. For one thing, they are all but unanimous in their support of the federal-city programs. They believe these programs have brought advantages to their cities which they would not otherwise have enjoyed—advantages expressed not only in social and aesthetic benefits but also in terms of economic gains. The new (or expanded) airports are held to have brought business to the cities, while center-city renovation not only has provided improved plant facilities but has resulted in increased tax revenue as well. Pittsburgh's Golden Triangle produces $2 million more each year in taxes than before its rehabilitation; the Front Street project in Rochester, New York, yields $400,000 more in taxes annually;[2] Little Rock's Urban Progress Association tells how six small individual residences were replaced by one apartment building with a consequent increase in taxes from $108 to $5,000 annually.[3] Not all reports are so favorable, but the sum of local sentiment is quite clear: the communities in general are more than satisfied with the new programs.

There is likewise almost unanimous approval of the direct relations that have sprung up between Washington and the cities. Virtually all city spokesmen, whether political leaders or administrators, find the direct channel from city hall to national capital agreeable; like Mayor Taft (quoted below), they would rather "do business" with the Washington agencies than with their state governments. This view is so generally held that it is not necessary to explore it further.

There is a corollary conviction, widely held, that the states have no proper or useful part to play in the prosecution of the new urban

mental relations. It was prepared by the staff of the Subcommittee on Intergovernmental Relations of the Committee on Government Operations, United States Senate, 88th Congress, 1st Session. These publications are useful for their corroborative testimony, but I have relied primarily on my own interview materials (as amplified by a mass of reports and records collected during the course of interviewing) for both the facts and the interpretations recorded here.

[2] "Urban Renewal," *Congressional Record*, vol. 107, no. 107, June 27, 1961.

[3] Urban Progress Association, "This is Progress!" (Little Rock, Arkansas: vol. V, no. III, August 10, 1964).

programs. It is recognized, of course, that they must provide enabling legislation, but beyond that community spokesmen place little reliance on state contributions. Community leaders in general are convinced that the states have no active interest in their problems, and that they lack the leadership, administrative organization, technical competence, and resources to make state participation in urban affairs meaningful. Those who express this view do not derogate state activities in such traditional fields as public education and highways, but confine their strictures to the thought of states sharing in the federal-city programs emphasized here. Of this, almost to a man, they want none.

Finally, community spokesmen are generally agreed on the subject of local organization, which they do not consider a factor critical to program success. There is general satisfaction, then, with the organizational pattern that exists in a community: other issues are held to be more important. Most local urban renewal and public housing programs are administered by separate agencies, as we have seen; most airports, on the other hand, are administered by a director appointed by the head of the city government. There is no widespread sense of a need to change in the direction of either integration or separation. An occasional mayor speaks grudgingly of the semi-autonomy enjoyed by the housing and renewal agencies, and a renewal or housing director now and then surmises that his agency may be sacrificing something through its isolation from the city government: a few, indeed, perceive that their insulation from municipal politics may not be without its risks. In the end, however, administrative organization is not regarded as of fundamental importance.

The local official, like the federal executive, can readily discover what relations between Washington and the cities are required by statute or manual. Also like his federal counterpart, he knows from observation and experience that a variety of factors, many of them fortuitous and some seemingly quite unrelated to program content, condition those relations in practice. Prominent among the conditioning factors is the local organization: its structure, its history of achievement (or the contrary), its relations with the city, the public support it enjoys, the strength of the authority board (where one exists), the role of politics in local activities, and so on. A companion consideration grows from the size and character of the city, which will reflect itself in the local program staff. A sizable community will be able to command the services of technically competent and experienced renewal, housing, and other program staffs. Its resources will be such as to permit and justify payment of specialists, so that the agency will have on its own staff many of the technicians it needs. A small community clearly has more need of federal staff assistance than does a large one; and the federal representatives may be expected to take into account variations in local needs notwithstanding the fact that the manual was designed to apply equally to all cities, great and small alike.

The direction taken by a particular program, and indeed the tone of the relations between a given city and the federal government, will depend largely on local leadership. In some cities political leadership is dominant; in others the professional staff, and more especially the program director, is paramount. Those conversant with the subject identify several kinds of local executives. First is the political leader, the mayor, who associates himself and his administration with a program, urban renewal, let us say, and stakes his political future on its success. Mayor Richard Lee of New Haven is a good example of this genus. Adventuresome and imaginative, he seeks new ways of employing urban renewal in the service of his city. His methods are direct and dramatic, and not always completely respectful of what he regards as bureaucratic procedures. An important urban renewal official spoke admiringly of Lee's achievements, which he pronounced spectacular, but reprovingly of his methods, which lay waste the manual of policies and requirements. Mayor Lee is doing a magnificent job, the federal official observed, but he could do just as good a job if he were a little less hell-bent and a little more observant of rules.

Second is the competent and experienced municipal executive without particularized program experience. The well-known manager of a large city symbolizes this category. A city manager of high repute, this individual nevertheless became entangled with the requirements of the Federal-Aid Airport Program. The district airport engineer wrote him a gently reproving letter setting forth in simple sequence the steps necessary to clear the matter up and bring the negotiations to successful conclusion. The manager, keenly conscious of the need for administrative regularity, retraced his steps, adopted the federal engineer's procedural recommendations, and all was well.

A third kind of local executive is the expansionist professional, of whom there are several around the country. These men have wide experience, and they enjoy national repute in their profession. Frequently they have served with the parent federal agency, in Washington, in the field, or sometimes both; they know the manual from cover to cover, some of them literally through experience in having helped write that document in the beginning. Such a man is Lawrence M. (Larry) Cox, executive director of the Norfolk Redevelopment and Housing Authority. Cox is characterized by the simplicity to be found on the far side of complexity: he has been "in the business" from his stripling days; he knows, or at one time did know, all the rules in the book "by heart"; over the years he has arrived at the enviable position where he does not have consciously to observe the regulations—Cox and the manual are one. His decisions are blandly assumed to be within the limits of the rules; the problem is not to suit the action to the rule book, but to find official justification for action desired to be taken or in some instances already taken, sometimes as long as three months or even six months before. As in the case of Mayor Lee, urban renewal officials speak respectfully of the results Larry Cox obtains but critically of the slam-bang methods he employs. Some years ago a management expert was added to Cox's staff (some say at the suggestion of the URA regional people), and since then less cause has been found for complaint.

A fourth type of local executive is found in the person of George A. McCulloch, until recently director of the Syracuse Office of Urban Renewal. McCulloch is reputed to have a boundless capacity for detail, along with considerable relish for the less exciting chores of administration. To report this judgment is not to suggest that he is therefore lacking in imagination, but only to suggest what all who know him affirm: that he is a complete master of the manual. Almost never does a paper submitted by McCulloch's office come back for further attention because of error in procedure or in factual detail. George McCulloch is the kind of local executive federal representatives like to deal with; with him they feel they can proceed direct to the merits of an issue without fear lest the papers not be in order.

These remarks suggest that the administration of federal-city programs revolves in considerable part around interpersonal relations. This is indeed the case, and community spokesmen know it well. For the most part they observe the rules as they understand them, but they never lose sight of the human factor. No policy, no regulation has meaning until individual, personal action has brought it to life. In the programs under discussion here the personal action in question is in good part professional: engineers deal with engineers, lawyers with lawyers, finance men with finance men. These men are interested in the technical aspects of the problem before them, and they bring common vocational bents and backgrounds to bear on its solution. It is only in moments of exasperation that they classify each other as "feds" and "locals." The professionals normally are absorbed in technical programmatic issues. The level of government at which a thing gets done is an incidental matter.

This is not so for the man whose primary involvement is with policy, as the mayor. His concern is for program achievements, not for a sound contract or for the scientific lighting of a runway. These are matters for the technicians; the mayor's interests are broader and longer, for he is a politician. Politicians are notorious shortcutters, with scant regard for administrative amenities. Such a man was Mayor W. F. Nicholson of Denver, who had strong White House ties in the late 1950s and who played them to the hilt in seeking to expedite FAA action on a proposal involving his city's airport. In so doing he alienated many FAA officials with responsibility for acting on the proposal. Mayor Nicholson did not deem it necessary to request the district airport engineer or the regional director for permission to confer with the President's staff. Nor for that matter did he consult the FAA Administrator, who frequently learned of the Mayor's Washington visits only after the fact. The feeling is general among those who know the facts that Mayor Nicholson may well have damaged rather than aided Denver's cause through his personal appeals to the White House.

Community leaders generally are sparing in their efforts to employ overt political pressure. An inquiry of an agency head by a member of Congress is considered normal, and that can usually be arranged without difficulty. Local program executives as a general rule are very careful to preserve good relations with federal representatives. This means consulting first with the federal people closest to the community, and moving up the ladder one step at a time and always with full notice along the way. Local executives uniformly maintain that they never "go to Washington" without the full knowledge of the district and regional officers. Interpersonal relations are the stuff of administration, but community spokesmen, both political and professional, understand that they must be practiced with discretion.

Basically the "expanded partnership" means intensified relations between the national government and the cities. The principal purpose of the federal government is to encourage local activities in selected program areas at a minimum standard of performance and at reasonable costs. It is the task of the city to choose the programs in which it wishes to participate and, with respect to each, to meet the requirements necessary to qualify for a grant-in-aid, and subsequently to conduct the program in question in such fashion as to continue to be eligible for assistance as long as the contract agreement shall run. The joining of these responsibilities entails a wide variety of close relations which may continue through many years. We have already identified a number of specific points of contact: preparation and review of applications for assistance, contractual relationships, field inspections by federal technicians, reports by local agencies, and so on. For present purposes three *kinds* of relations have been chosen for discussion. These are the "workable program" now required by all constituent divisions of the Housing and Home Finance Agency which deal directly with the communities; the manual of operations used by all federal agencies, which contains the rules and regulations governing program conduct; and the audit, which in a variety of guises is performed by all federal agencies that support local grant-in-aid programs.

The workable program, as noted in the previous chapter, originated in the requirement that a city applying for a grant for urban renewal must have a plan. In the beginning the requirement was not of particular significance because the plan submitted by the city was frequently so general and so superficial as to be without real value, and because the Urban Renewal Administration as a matter of practice certified as acceptable almost any plan the city might choose to submit. Further, the process of annual recertification failed to realize its potential value when the URA adopted the practice of recertifying almost as a matter of course. Finally, the requirement of a plan was limited to the urban renewal program.

In the course of time the minimal requirement that the city produce a plan was broadened and strengthened in several ways. The requirement of a city plan became one for a workable program for community development instead. The workable program concept requires the city to look toward community improvement in the broadest sense, and the program must include component elements each of which is designed to make a specific contribution to the program as a whole. The workable program in a sense remains a plan, but a variform plan marking paths toward progress along a multiple front. The requirement compels the city to examine with care its total needs and aspirations, to weigh its resources against its goals, and to explore the steps necessary to close the gap between the two. The urban renewal program is, of course, conceived as one of the principal devices for closing the gap. Also, the workable program received more careful attention in Washington than did the general plan earlier required. It is analyzed and evaluated with care by technicians, and the HHFA Administrator himself must indicate the agency's satisfaction by signifying his approval of the program. Again, the process of annual recertification, once almost automatic, has become increasingly rigorous over the last few years. Further, the workable program, originally limited to cities seeking urban renewal assistance, has been extended to the other divisions of the Housing and Home Finance Agency as well so that it is now (where applicable) an agency-wide requirement. The workable program signalizes a growing awareness on the part of the HHFA that it cannot limit its concern for the city to narrowly circumscribed, individual programs, but that it must consider problems of the community in their totality and try to bring all its resources to bear on those problems. The effort is not very far advanced and it is not particularly well articulated, but a promising start has been made.

Some program executives accept the workable program requirement simply as a task to be done, but many welcome it as offering an opportunity and a challenge. These individuals know, of course, that there are sharp variations in quality from one workable program to another; they know that there is an occasional community which gives its workable program casual thought in the first instance and minimal attention thereafter. But public housing and urban renewal executives are convinced of the long-range utility of planning, and they regard the workable program as the community's chief hope for planning in a broad and inclusive sense. Consequently they give almost uniform support to the workable program concept, whatever shortcomings it may reveal occasionally in local practice.

A second kind of relation between Washington and the cities springs from the manual of policies and requirements. All three of the federal agencies whose programs are examined here have such manuals; and all set high store by them, for they define the policies and set out the regulations under which local bodies (agencies, authorities, sponsors) operate. By the same token they describe the relations that shall prevail between the federal government and the localities, insofar as these relations can be spelled out in writing.

The manual of any federal agency sets forth general policies and procedures applicable throughout the country. The principal requirement of a manual, indeed, is that its provisions be of such nature as to be generally applicable to all situations and in all places. Actually, of course, the various federal-city programs would grind to a halt quickly if the rules of the manual were applied literally and without regard for local conditions. The local executive knows this well. Thus while some directors will accept without question a ruling made by a federal representative, the more resourceful ones will press for flexibility in interpretation and application. They will search for tolerances in the rules and will probe their limits.

We observed earlier that there are many factors contributing to a lack of uniformity in the application of manual rules. One federal agency will regard its manual as sacrosanct, another will consider it nothing more than a general guide toward program execution. One administrator, holding a tight rein on his program, will require a strict interpretation of manual provisions; another, pursuing an expansionist course, will encourage a loose construction. Men inevitably interpret and apply the rules in different ways in different circumstances, even when given the same set of instructions for the use of the manual. Younger officials are more likely to be strict in their interpretations than are older and more experienced ones. Thus the most unswerving application of the rules is to be found in the field offices, the less rigid interpretations toward the top of the administrative ladder. The field representative may understand this, yet feel he has no option but to "follow the book." Such a representative may view an appeal from an adverse ruling with a sense of relief. Local executives have reported instances of tacit encouragement by a regional representative to carry an appeal to Washington.

This brings us to further consideration of the factor of personal relations in administration. Such relations are at the center of the administrative process; given the general pattern of operations set forth in the manual, they supply the element of flexibility that makes a program workable. They rest upon a variety of considerations: professional respect, demonstrated competence, reputation for integrity, personal friendship—all these and perhaps, occasionally, some baser ones as well. The emphasis here is on the *man* rather than the *manual*.

The director of a local public agency in a large midwestern city reports a case showing how flexibility enters into the interpretation of the manual. A representative of the regional office, a planner, had taken exception to a proposal made by the director, who appealed to the regional office. There the URA regional director became a party to the discussion, which ended when he said to the planner: "You don't like the proposal because it does not reflect sound planning, but that's not enough to condemn it in my book. Let 'em have it, if it's not illegal; after all, —— is their city." A similar incident concerned a traffic light that had been installed at a point where a road passed near the end of an airfield runway; it was in want of an operator. The solution seemed simple enough: let the control tower operate the traffic light. This, however, was against the regulations, yet no other solution appeared feasible. In the end this was the solution arrived at, with the regional administrator wagging his finger at the airport manager in a letter ending with this sentence: "As a matter of record, we are opposed to the use of particular traffic lights except in unusual cases, of which this is, in our opinion, one." Another instance still reflects a somewhat firmer tone. The executive director of the housing authority in a large city made a proposal regarding a housing project for the elderly which met the approval of his commission but which failed to win the assent of the regional office. Local negotiation failed to resolve the difficulty, and the executive director, with the approval of his board, appealed the regional ruling to Washington. On appeal, he found himself presently talking to the PHA commissioner. There was a prolonged conversation, which ended on this exchange: "Mr. Commissioner, this is what we are going to do, if we do anything; and if you cannot go along with us on this, you know what you can do with your d——d project." After a few seconds of silence, the commissioner replied: "Okay, ——, build 'em your way; but don't come back here for any more money." "That's an agreement," the executive director rejoined. "We will build 'em our way, and we will not ask you for additional money."

Notwithstanding these and many like evidences of flexibility in interpreting or applying manual procedures, the feeling is widespread among local program executives that the manual is applied with too little regard for special situations. One local executive complains of the delay in approving change orders, which frequently leads to increased costs through suspension of work during construction. Another relates that he was required to provide a photograph of a sign in place before a project. The project was so far along that the sign had been taken down and stored. He put the sign back in place and had a photographer come out and "shoot" the scene. "I am just waiting to see whether the photographer's charge will get past the auditors," he concluded. Still another local executive takes exception to the handling of contracts. Every proposed contract must have the approval of the regional office; this we accept, he says, because the manual requires it. But the regional office keeps each contract between two and three months, and when it comes back to us changes frequently will have been made in minute detail: individual words will have been changed, new phraseology inserted, punctuation corrected, and so on. "We do not believe this is necessary," he maintains with some heat, "and more than that we do not believe the manual requires such detailed editing."

There is almost universal criticism of the federal agencies on the ground of delay. Delays of two to three months in handling even routine matters are regarded as normal. A classic example is provided by the efforts of Denver to gain the support of the FAA for a new jet-plane runway. Three long years dragged out between the initiation of this effort and its successful conclusion. In this case, however, responsibility for the delay was by no means to be attributed exclusively to the Federal Aviation Agency. For one thing, Denver did not know in the beginning just what it wanted, and so got off to a number of false starts. For another, the decision was an extraordinarily complicated one, involving as it did the acquisition of several hundred acres of surplus land from a nearby U.S. Army installation and involving further the neighboring city of Aurora. For still another, the mayor of Denver muddied the water by attempting to inject political pressure into what was essentially a complex technical problem. There was also the matter of a popular referendum on a proposed bond issue to finance airport development. All in all, then, the total elapsed time may not have been unreasonable, though the Denver people could see only that it had taken three years to get FAA approval for construction of a runway.

The former executive director of the housing authority of a large southwestern city relates the harrowing details of an effort to build a high-rise home for the elderly. Like the Denver airport project, this effort covered a three-year span. The proceedings reached crisis proportions when, with construction well along, the PHA regional office conducted a post review and took exception to the architect-engineering specifications on fourteen counts. The local board responded by accepting two and rejecting twelve of the regional director's directed changes. The information available does not indicate where the merits in this controversy lay, though it may be presumed that (a) the regional director was within the limits of manual requirements in ordering "corrections" which (b) the local housing authority considered unreasonable and unnecessary. In any event, the project was completed without important modifications and with federal support. Presumably similar controversies will be avoided in the future by reason of changes introduced by the erstwhile local executive director, who has moved up to the post of commissioner of the Public Housing Administration.

By way of general comment on the manual, there is abundant evidence of uneven application of its policy guides and requirements in times past. There is also evidence of a disposition in recent years to take a more positive view of the manual and the purposes to be served by it. More than one agency has revised its manual to provide for both a briefer and a more general catalogue of regulations. A manual's true goal is of course to facilitate rather than obstruct action. There is promise that this goal will be sought increasingly as the federal-city programs gain in experience, assurance, and stature.

A third kind of relation between Washington agencies and the communities grows out of the audit and auditing procedure. Each agency has an audit or system of audits designed to serve its own needs. Each has an annual fiscal audit designed to ensure a proper accounting for federal funds. In addition, some federal agencies have periodic program and management reviews which, whether or not audits in a technical sense, are thought of as audits and are so called by the local program executives. The Public Housing Administration, as the federal agency with perhaps the closest and certainly the most extended relations with the community, possesses the most varied system of audits.

A recent "Consolidated Review of Management Operations of the Norfolk Redevelopment and Housing Authority," prepared by the Washington regional office of the Public Housing Administration, covered these subjects: operations analysis, management, occupancy, insurance-taxation, personal property, fiscal management, operations engineering, utilities, accounting, and audit. A "management audit" is made every three to five years. It requires three or four months of work in the office, and during this time specialists from the regional office come and go at frequent intervals. When the auditors have finished their work, a conference is arranged with appropriate local staff members for a general discussion of the findings about to be reported. At this point errors in fact may be corrected and emphases in interpretations modified in the light of local reactions. After some weeks a copy of the review report comes down from the regional office, and the local director sets about the business of answering the criticisms made there. His answers will usually satisfy the regional criticisms on a few points, leaving the bulk to be dealt with through changes ("corrections") in local practices. In Norfolk, one man is given the responsibility for following through on the necessary corrections. Occasional exchanges gradually reduce the area of difference between regional office and local authority, but now and then a regional criticism will remain unsatisfied for two years or longer. It is quite clear that the regional office sets great store by its occasional management review, and that the local authority gives high priority to the matter of satisfying the criticisms made in the review. Examination of PHA management review procedures in both Denver and Philadelphia substantiates this conclusion.

Federal auditing of local accounts and procedures has few critics *in principle*. Even the most ardent advocate of local autonomy recognizes the right, indeed the obligation, of federal agencies to keep a reasonably close watch over local programs that are supported by federal funds. Many local program executives feel, however, that federal auditing goes far beyond what is necessary or reasonable. Here is how the PHA system of audits looks to one local director:

> Gradually PHA has, through the years, intensified and expanded its control and domination of local affairs. This has been done through intensified audits of every conceivable nature: audits of management, audits of tenant reports, audits of maintenance activities, audits of the fiscal books of account, audits of community-tenant programs, audits of filing systems, audits of public relations, audits on top of audits—not necessarily to improve, to suggest, or to correct, but to criticize, to dominate, and to find fault—to press all local authorities into the same mold.[4]

Another local director recently reported that in the course of nine months he had had twenty-three different auditors, inspectors, super-

[4] Personal letter to the author, September 9, 1960.

visors, and compliance men from the PHA and the URA in his office. These auditors, he continued, even though personally pleasant and agreeable nevertheless cause a great deal of confusion. They require work space, and space usually is in short supply. They preempt the files while they are on hand and on departure leave them in a state of disarray. By law this must be endured, he concluded, but it could be borne with better grace if the questions asked by the auditors were confined to important subjects. Cracks in the sidewalk, rat holes under the steps, warped doors, spots denuded of grass—numerous items of this kind find their way into audit reports. Local executives maintain they have no proper place there.

The discussion to this point concerns agency audit and review. The General Accounting Office (GAO) conducts an occasional audit (perhaps not oftener than once in five to eight years) of a particular local authority. The GAO audit is the cause of profound dissatisfaction and sharp criticism among virtually all local directors. As they describe it, this audit subjects the local authority to grave inconvenience and yields few positive results. A sizable local agency will be visited by a team of at least half a dozen auditors, who may require as long as four months for completion of their work. They are "pure" auditors in the sense that they know little of the authority's program, hence have to be educated from scratch. The GAO auditor's approach is mechanical rather than programmatic. His orientation is indicated by the question that provides his guideline regarding any particular action: "Was this step taken in compliance with the manual and does it meet the requirements of the law?" Not all local directors interviewed have been subjected to a GAO audit, but not one who has thought it a justifiable expenditure of money or time. They do not believe that Congress can acquire a grasp of their programs nationally from a general report based on the individual GAO audits with which they are acquainted.

In summary, those who view the federal audit and review system from the community level find that it leaves much to be desired. They do not believe that the GAO audit serves any constructive purpose, and they resent it as a needless imposition. Concerning agency audits they feel that the audit has been used for centralizing control at the expense of local autonomy, and also that the several audits are repetitious and therefore unnecessarily demanding of time. Their recommendations for the improvement of auditing procedure are:

1. Eliminate the GAO audit. (The local directors are not naive enough to suppose this can or will be done.)

2. Limit the audit to considerations of regularity of accounts and compatibility of local policy with national policy. They feel that most of the detailed matters now covered should be left to local determination.

3. Combine the various audits into a general once-and-for-all audit which all federal agencies with local concerns would then accept. These specific goals may be beyond attainment, but translated into a plea for relevance in audits and simplicity in auditing procedures they would seem to warrant serious consideration.

As those who speak for the community view federal-local relations, three principal problems seem worthy of emphasis. The first concerns the issue of centralization versus decentralization *within* the federal structure. It has to do with the relations between the headquarters and the field officers of the several program agencies. An illustration of the problem is provided by the Federal Aviation Agency. The American Association of Airport Executives and its members supported the creation of the FAA in 1958, expecting that the new agency would be more sympathetic to airport needs than was its predecessor. Their expectations were quickly frustrated, however, by the head of the new agency. On the one hand, they report, General Quesada proved unsympathetic toward the Federal-Aid Airport Program, while on the other he moved forthwith to centralize the power of decision in his office in Washington. This effectively undermined both regional and district offices as decision-making centers. The district airport engineer, on whom the airport executives generally had learned to rely for answers to fairly important questions, suddenly lost his voice, as did his immediate superior, the regional director. The questions and the men who received them were the same after 1958 as before, but the authority to provide answers had been removed from the field to Washington. And in Washington, General Quesada proved inaccessible. Local program executives do not always get answers to their questions, nor do they always get the answers they want, from federal field representatives; but they prefer a system under which wide power of decision is vested in field officers. The trend toward decentralization, in evidence since 1960, therefore meets with their complete approval.

Another problem concerns the balance between local autonomy and federal control. This indeed is the central issue implicit in local dissatisfaction with the interpretation and application of manual regulations and with auditing procedures. The gist of the complaint on both counts is that the manual and the audit are employed for the purposes of centralizing control, inducing conformity, and minimizing decision-making at the community level. The view favored by the local executives is accurately summarized in the position of the regional official quoted above: "Let 'em have it, if it's not illegal. After all, it's their city."

A surprising (and undoubtedly growing) number of community leaders identified metropolitanism as a third major problem. The familiar argument is heard time and time again: our problems are not confined to the city, and it is folly to treat them as if they were; what is required is a metropolitan government (or agency) to deal with problems which know no local legal boundaries. It is not necessary to pursue the point further at this time. What is important is that a great many community spokesmen, including local program executives, know something of the metropolitan problem and are convinced that "something has to be done about it."

In final analysis, what we have called here the "expanded partnership" consists essentially in the public recognition and marked extension of cooperative federalism. The practice of modern federalism entails intricate relations among governments; and as governments expand their activities in new and untried directions, intergovernmental relations grow in both number and complexity. Community spokesmen, and particularly program executives, are inclined not to pay sufficient heed to the complexity of government, and so to the process of decision-making, in the modern world. Urban government itself is far from simple: involved in one internal negotiation covering the Norfolk airport were the city manager, the city attorney, the engineer, the general manager of the Norfolk Port and Industrial Authority, and the NPIA general counsel. At the federal level, a Washington meeting called to consider a development at the Denver airport was attended by the entire Colorado congressional delegation, several representatives of the city, two FAA officials, four spokesmen for the Army, three for the Air Force, and one for the National Guard. One of the points at issue in this deliberation was the highly secret, and highly dangerous, work being done by the Army Chemical Corps at the adjoining military installation—work of which Denver had known almost nothing when it proposed to construct a runway that would bring planes in and send them out over the Army's chemical plant. A number of factors contributed to the delay that Denver experienced in straightening out its runway problem, but a chief contributor was the necessity of negotiating agreement among several governments and their agents.

To say that relations among governments, particularly governments at different levels, are necessarily complex is not to say that they cannot be systematized and in some measure simplified. Federal agencies and their programs can be more effectively coordinated, the manual can be condensed and clarified, auditing procedures can be tightened up, the metropolitan problem can be alleviated through attack from a number of promising directions. Even after all this is done, however, the complexities of intergovernmental relations will remain, for complexity is an inescapable accompaniment of modern government.

THE STATE HOUSE: THE MIDWAY VIEW

Federalism has of course meant different things to different men in different eras; but never has it portended, to any more than a handful of frightened men, the eclipse of the states. It is perhaps laboring the obvious to observe that in our federal system the position of the states for almost two centuries has been thought secure.

What, then, of their position in the expanded federal system? In particular, what of their role with respect to the new federal-city programs? The states not unnaturally supposed they would be called upon to play an important part in the administration of programs designed to meet the problems of the new urban world. And so they were. Many a call has been issued over the course of two decades for positive, imaginative action by the states in response to the growing concentration in population and its attendant problems. As a single illustration, Carter McFarland, then a high official in the Housing and Home Finance Agency, in 1959 wrote an article entitled "Urban Renewal: An Opportunity for the States."[5] There he directed attention to the potential significance of state action, and listed a number of steps the states might take to make their influence felt in the growing field of urban renewal. Three years later *The Wall Street Journal* reported optimistically that the governors were planning moves which would permit the states to meet their obligations in our increasingly urban world. "Help for Cities: States Step Up Efforts to Solve Growing Problems," the *Journal* proclaimed.[6]

The fruits of these and many like exhortations have been assessed, for the most part by implication, in Chapter 3. Let us therefore summarize. In the article cited, McFarland listed five steps the states might take to establish themselves as serious partners in the attack on urban blight:

1. Create a state agency for urban renewal.
2. Review and perfect enabling legislation.
3. Provide leadership and technical assistance to localities.
4. Assist localities in developing and enforcing housing standards.
5. Provide financial assistance to localities.

Most states have followed the author's recommendation with respect to item 2; regarding the other recommended measures there has been an almost unbroken silence. A few states have chosen to participate actively in urban redevelopment, as we have seen; but for the most part the states have remained quiescent in the face of this challenge. And in the face of most of the others as well. Regarding the new programs designed to alleviate the metro-problems born of the last two decades, the states have pursued pretty much a hands-

[5] *State Government*, vol. XXXII, no. 3 (Summer 1959), pp. 193–198.
[6] *The Wall Street Journal*, vol. LXVII, no. 1 (June 2, 1962), p. 1.

off policy. They have manifested little desire to be drawn into the urbanism vortex.

There are those observers who trace state lassitude in the metro-urban field to the federal-city programs themselves, and more especially to the early federal decisions to emphasize direct relations with the cities. Once this system had been established, the reasoning goes, the states not only were eliminated from meaningful administrative participation in the programs but were also, by clear implication, excused from responsibility regarding them. There were other important things for the states to do—in the fields of education, welfare, and highways, for example—and they proceeded to do them, leaving to the federal government and the cities the problem areas of which we treat here. It was inevitable, the argument continues, that the states should one day find it necessary to take an active part in dealing with the newer urban problems. That day is now here, and the states are in truth awakening to the obligations which are inescapably theirs in the breakneck society of urban America. That they have not done so before is in good part explainable by the fact that they were not required to confront the metropolitan challenge as they were forced to meet that of road building, for example, fifty years ago.

Their spectator role has not of course prevented the states from adopting a critical attitude with regard to both the substance of the programs and the procedures employed in their execution. State spokesmen dwell upon two issues which they identify as characteristic of current trends on the one hand and as threats to states' rights on the other. The first, the issue of centralization, is viewed as being inherent in the grant-in-aid system. Frederick Mosher has argued that the data available, objectively analyzed and interpreted, indicate that there is in fact a moderate trend toward *de*centralization. Objectivity, however, is not one of the strong points of the most vigorous critics of recent trends: the federal government collects and spends more money than the states and its debt is larger, therefore there is, *ipso facto*, centralization.

Centralization, the reasoning goes, has come about over the last three decades through two major developments. First, the federal government has "pre-empted" the most lucrative sources of

public revenue, leaving to the states a few ragtag-and-bobtail sources
from which only modest revenues can be derived. Second, the federal government has intruded into functional fields reserved to the
states by the Constitution. In effect, the charge is that the federal
government has expropriated state tax sources to support programs
wrested from state hands by superior force. The states as a result
are withering away. To the states' righter the remedy is simple:
Let the federal government "return" to the states the functions which
"rightfully" belong to them, and let the national government at the
same time "turn back" to the states the lucrative revenue sources
previously pre-empted. The argument sometimes takes on a ring of
outrage, as in the opening strains of a resolution adopted February
2, 1963, by the Board of Directors of the North Carolina Association
of County Commissioners:

> WHEREAS, County officials know from bitter experience that the
> federal government places heavy restrictions on state and local activi-
> ties where federal grants-in-aid are involved, which restrictions re-
> duce the area of decision of state and local officials and increase the
> cost of these activities, . . .

The argument rests upon two notable concepts that are implicit
in the words "pre-emption" (as applied to revenue sources) and
"return" (as applied to public functions). Pre-emption appears to
consist in the adoption of certain taxes by the federal government
before the states were ready to adopt them. It is not clear in what
sense this constitutes pre-emption, nor is it clear that the states
would be prepared to move in with equivalent levies in the event
the Congress should vacate these taxes. The word "return" suggests
that the federal government seized certain functions which the
states were pursuing at the time of seizure, and that this wrong
could be righted by handing the functions over to the states, which
would be both glad to receive them and able and willing to carry
them along.

Passing by the concepts themselves, the remedial measures
proposed are open to serious question. Would the states in fact be
prepared to levy new taxes in the event the Congress should decide
to eliminate the federal taxes most in controversy? There is grave
doubt that such a result would follow. Many states have constitu-

tional limitations that would make impossible state imposition of the taxes in question. States are in competition with one another for industry and commerce, as we have noted in another connection, and new taxes might affect adversely a state's competitive position; any new state tax, indeed, would be certain to encounter this charge. States generally are unwilling to levy new taxes or increase old ones from political considerations, and there is no reason to suppose that any action the federal government might take would appreciably modify this attitude. Some taxes could not be administered successfully by the states. Finally, if all went well in the matter of federal vacation and state imposition of taxes on lucrative sources, the state legislatures, heavily weighted in favor of rural interests as they have been in the past, could be expected to continue to slight metro-urban problems in favor of the mitigation of rural and small-town pressures.

This brings into question the wisdom of "returning" the federal-city programs to the states. Perhaps it is not charitable, however true, to call attention to the fact that not more than a few states have ever assumed significant program responsibilities in these areas, but it is no more than fair to require evidence of good faith of those who advocate "returning" programmatic responsibilities to the states. Such evidence would be hard to produce. For the states have been slow to take meaningful hold of urban problems in the past, and there is little sign of any real intention to do so now. It is significant that few urban spokesmen are willing even to discuss the possibility of shifting responsibility for such programs as urban renewal, airport development, public housing, mass transit, and pollution abatement from the federal government to the states, and fewer still regard such a shift as desirable. The view of the city people is summed up succinctly in an exchange that took place at a House committee hearing in 1957.

> Mr. Dawson: Do you think that these grant-in-aid programs of the Government would fare better if they were turned over to the States?
>
> Mayor Taft (of Cincinnati): They would disappear.

A little later another aspect of the problem came up in this exchange:

Mr. Dawson: You would rather do business with the Federal Government?

Mayor Taft: I would rather do business with Washington, and don't tell me I am being a New Dealer when I say that.[7]

A second major issue pressed by spokesmen for the states concerns what they regard as the perversion of the federal system through direct relations between Washington and the cities. In question is the role of the states with respect to the urban programs. Seen in one light, these programs could provide a potent stimulant to flagging state energies; seen in another, they pose a grave threat to the sovereignty of the states.

The federal-state highway program is thought by the states to rest upon sound practice. That program, it will be recalled, maximizes the role of the states; for on the one hand they receive vast sums of money from the federal government, and on the other they bear a major responsibility for the construction and maintenance of roads in the federal-state highway system. Symptomatic of this view is a bill introduced into the House of Representatives at the behest of the National Association of State Aviation Officials which would revise federal-aid airport program procedures "to conform more closely with those of the federal-aid highway program." Among other things, the bill would provide for a general aviation system, and would vest its planning and development in the state aviation agencies.[8]

Many advocates of the new urban programs take a contrary view of the role of the states. Some insist that the states have no interest or competence in the domain of metropolitan problems, that they possess inadequate resources for dealing with those problems, and therefore there is no significant place for the states in the programs in question. Most mayors, for example, would simply eliminate the states from significant consideration in program development or administration; like Mayor Taft, they prefer to deal with Washington.

[7] Hearings before a Subcommittee of the Committee on Government Operations, House of Representatives, 85th Congress, 1st Session, *Federal-State-Local Relations, State and Local Officials,* Part 2 (1958), pp. 611, 614.

[8] A. B. McMullen, "Aviation among the States," in *The Book of the States, 1964–1965,* pp. 374–377.

The word "channeling" symbolizes the issue. The question is whether federal funds for urban programs should be channeled through the state or made available to the cities direct. In the first instance the states at most could exert considerable influence, and at the least would not feel snubbed. In the second, their role would be minimized, for the meaningful relations would be those between Washington and the cities. Virtually all state spokesmen support the channeling of federal funds through state agencies. Actually they desire to see the highway program arrangement invoked in the case of each federal-city program. In the prevailing circumstances they are generally willing to accept channeling as a substitute, although they regard it as a poor one. Almost all city spokesmen resist the channeling of federal funds for local programs through the states. They consider such a procedure a waste of time and a bother, especially because they foresee an additional layer of procedural requirements if channeling is made uniform and if the states decide to force recognition of its implication. This quarrel goes back many years. The controversy was examined with some care and adequately summarized in Chapter 4.

Recently the Advisory Commission on Intergovernmental Relations entered the lists in behalf of state channeling with this statement:

> The Commission recommends that the States assume their proper responsibilities for assisting and facilitating urban development; to this end it is recommended that Federal grants-in-aid to local governments for urban development be channeled through the States in cases where a State (a) provides appropriate administrative machinery to carry out relevant responsibilities and (b) provides significant financial contributions, and when appropriate, technical assistance to the local governments concerned.[9]

[9] *Impact of Federal Urban Development Programs on Local Government Organizations and Planning,* Prepared in Cooperation with the Subcommittee on Intergovernmental Relations of the Committee on Government Operations, United States Senate, by the Advisory Commission on Intergovernmental Relations (88th Congress, 2d Session; Committee Print, May 30, 1964), p. 30. Pages 30–33 of this report afford a good summary of the channeling issue. The ACIR employs "urban development" here to comprehend all programs "which (1) culminate in physical construction activity, and . . . which (2) involve planning for the physical development of urban communities and their urban-rural fringes" (p. 1).

It is of interest to note that the commission hedged its recommendation in provisos (a) and (b), which evidently are designed to stimulate state action. It would appear that not more than three or four states would qualify to receive federal grants in aid for urban development under the above recommendation. It is notable, too, that the recommendation did not command unanimous support in the commission; on the contrary, it was adopted by a majority of one vote, with all representatives of the cities voting No. Senator Edmund S. Muskie (Maine), chairman of the Senate Subcommittee on Intergovernmental Relations and ACIR member, summarized the negative view in these words:

> In my opinion, federalism does not require that all levels of government be involved in every program of joint action. A uniform administrative pattern for channeling all Federal funds for urban-related programs, moreover, would undermine the flexibility that has contributed so greatly to the success of these programs. The failure of many States to develop an understanding of and sympathy with these cooperative efforts must not be overlooked.[10]

In conclusion, it is clear that the states view the growing practice of federal-city relations with disfavor and distrust. They are critical of the grant-in-aid system in general on the ground that it results in a centralized federal government which threatens the well-being if not the existence of the states. They are even more critical of the growing practice of direct dealing between Washington and the cities, which they regard as both a perversion of the federal system and a pointed threat to state sovereignty. Inasmuch as most states have manifested little concern for the problems at which the federal-city programs are aimed, the chief casualty of the expanded federalism would appear to be state pride. It is not that the states wish to play an active role, but that they wish to be thought of as wishing to. Perhaps they even wish to think of themselves as wishing to.

[10] *Ibid.,* p. 31.

7.

The Expanded Partnership:
Appraisal

We have seen how the American federal system came to be expanded to include the cities as a third partner. We have seen, too, something of the nature of the expanded partnership, and we have examined the views held by the participants. It remains to appraise the new, three-level federal system. What consequences have followed in the wake of the amplified federalism? What problems have risen from its practice? What is its significance for democratic government? Because the federal system does not stand still for description and evaluation, the answers to these and like questions must be couched in tentative, even speculative, terms. It is the purpose of this chapter to explore the three questions asked by way of appraisal, if only tentative appraisal, of the expanded federal system.

CONSEQUENCES ANTICIPATED AND UNANTICIPATED

Of the identifiable consequences of the expanded federalism, some are direct and intended, others incidental and proximate. A principal consequence has been explicit recognition of the vast and complex problems of metro-America as problems of concern to all America. Acceptance of this view was indeed prerequisite to national action, hence it may be more truly identified as a precondition than as a result. However classified, the indisputable fact is that gradually

171

over the last three decades, in a fits-and-starts development that sometimes obscured the trend, the national government has emerged as a vigorous participant in the attack on public problems long held to be "local" in character. There was a time in truth when the view of housing, blight, transit, water and air pollution, and the like as local problems could be defended with a show of logic. That view became less and less tenable with the progressive urbanization of America; and as urbanism merged into metropolism and the latter grew from a torrent to a flood, all semblance of reason left the ancient tradition. Such problems palpably are not local, nor are they indeed urban except in distant origin, for they have outgrown both locality and community, even expanded community. They are, on the contrary, *public* in nature, and the public involved is nothing less than the American people. They are therefore national problems; and if their place of origin is the metropolis they remain nonetheless national in both scope and significance. The first conclusion to be drawn is that this lesson has been learned and its implications accepted by all, by the people and by the governments involved alike.

Second, the expanded federalism reflects recognition of the need to match public problems with public resources. "Resources" are sometimes thought to include chiefly (or only) money. Beyond money, however, are resources which for want of a better term we may call human. They inhere in the perspective which permits men of vision and experience to see that a problem exists, the imagination to speculate on possible solutions, the political wisdom and skill to fashion public policies, and the administrative capacity to carry the resultant programs into effect. Such resources are not distributed across the face of the country by geographic areas or governmental entities, any more than fiscal resources are so distributed. It is idle to say that a particular community does not have the resources to deal with a given problem; for it has been demonstrated conclusively that public resources are available to deal with any serious and insistent public problem wherever found. The federal government has long been the only agency for marshaling revenues and allocating expenditures on a national scale. The expanded grant-in-aid programs have had the collateral effect of nationalizing also such human attributes as education, experience, and expertise. There is no longer need for any city to suffer for want of knowledge, imagination, or perspective with relation to any of the federal-local programs. This nationalization—it tends to become equalization—of resources may be as important a consequence of the amplified federalism as any.

A companion result is found in the approach to uniform standards throughout the nation. For every program Congress has set basic standards, while leaving their elaboration to the appropriate administrative agency. In every instance the agency involved has expanded the minimum standards into a network of specifications, procedures, inspections, and reports designed to standardize and make uniform program performance. These apply at all levels of activity: in Washington, in the regional offices, in the cities where the programs take physical form. Such standards not only ensure uniformity of procedure but also serve to build a floor under performance, so that activity of a minimum quality will emerge throughout the country. It is sometimes argued that homogeneity is but another word for monotony, that public housing looks like public housing wherever it is observed, that no flexibility is left for adaptation to local conditions. The preceding chapter dealt implicitly with the charge of overstandardization. At this point it may be sufficient to observe that the airlines welcome the uniformity which ensures that their pilots will bring their planes down on scientifically constructed runways, whether in Philadelphia or in Great Falls.

Another significant consequence of the amplified federalism flows from the general upgrading of urban government. To illustrate, the city has been invited to undertake important programs which it might otherwise have passed by. Also, cities generally have been compelled by the requirements mentioned above to make careful surveys of their needs, to take thorough inventories of their assets, and to devise detailed plans for closing the gap. The most notable illustration is that provided by the Housing and Home Finance Agency's requirement of a "workable program," which has encouraged, indeed compelled, cities to conduct self-surveys as prerequisites to program proposals. In so doing it has greatly strengthened the role of the planners, although this was not its primary intent. By the same token, likewise as a by-product, it has joined with other devices of federal oversight measurably to strengthen city government.

The principal purpose of the new grant-in-aid programs was, of course, the amelioration of metro-urban problems—problems identified as urban in origin but national in impact: public housing, urban renewal, airport development, mass transit, pollution control, and the like. Notwithstanding an occasional dissenting opinion, the consensus is that the several programs have made promising progress toward achievement of their announced goals. The record of physical accomplishment (summarized in Chapter 5) is impressive; and those most directly involved, the spokesmen of the cities, speak virtually with one voice in approving the existing programs and urging more. Cynics ask, "Why should not the cities approve a program which brings them two or three outside dollars for every local dollar invested?" Realists reply, "Why should they not indeed, since the federal-aid programs offer the hope—the only hope they have discovered—of being able, with help, to deal effectively with problems which but recently seemed overpowering?" To the cities, the progress they have made under the federal-aid programs is substantial, and they will countenance no proposal for any important modification.

Finally, in refrain of a theme announced earlier, the federal-local grant programs have resulted in a marked growth in the practice of cooperative federalism. One kind of evidence is found in the increasing relations among governments at all levels, and in recent official recognition of the significance of intergovernmental relations. The Commission on Intergovernmental Relations of the mid-1950s was the harbinger of this trend, the establishment of the Advisory Commission on Intergovernmental Relations and of intergovernmental relations subcommittees of the appropriate congressional committees its principal fruits.

Further evidence is found in the increasing traffic on the road to Washington. A third of a century ago only an occasional mayor made his way to the nation's capital; now a count made on a given day would disclose the presence there of perhaps a score, and that number can swell to a hundred within a few hours when a subject of concern to the cities comes up for discussion. A number of cities keep representatives in Washington, either individually or jointly with other cities. Organizations representing the urban areas now maintain headquarters in Washington—the American Municipal Association, the United States Conference of Mayors, and the National Association of Counties, to name but three.[1] It must be remembered that the road to Washington is not a one-way street; on the contrary, Washington officials not only are available for technical consultation but frequently "take their story" to the cities on their own initiative. "Washington" is not Washington alone, but also the many regional and distinct office cities, where hundreds of federal representatives maintain a lively intercourse with the cities as their principal responsibility. There is no way to measure the increased relations between Washington and the cities in quantitative terms, but observation warrants the speculation that it may have increased perhaps a thousand times since 1932.

The expansion of the federal system from a two- to a three-way partnership stands as the principal incidental consequence of the growth of federal-city relations. Neither the federal government nor the cities sought consciously to expand the sweep of federalism, but instead sought only to deal more effectively with problems beyond the scope or resources of traditional governments operating within customary and long-standing usage. This was in the best tradition of American pragmatism. What has emerged is an expanded system which reveals American federalism once more as a tough, resilient, flexible institution capable of adapting to conditions and complexities unforeseen by the founders. If de Tocqueville could pay us a return visit, he would be more than ever "struck by the good sense and practical judgment of the Americans . . . in the ingenious devices by which they elude the numberless difficulties resulting from their federal Constitution."

[1] A useful summary of "Representation of Metropolitan Interests in Washington" appears as Chapter 2 in Robert H. Connery and Richard H. Leach, *The Federal Government and Metropolitan Areas* (Cambridge, Mass.: Harvard University Press, 1960).

PROBLEMS REAL AND FANCIED

The growth of direct, open, and continued relations between the federal government and the cities has brought in its train certain problems. Many of these are fancied but some are real. Of the real problems, some are exaggerated by occasional observers beyond reason or justification. Others are common to novel developments in a complex and fluxing field, and require continuing attention on the part of the policy-makers. Three significant problems have been chosen for discussion here. They concern local government organization for administering the federal-city programs, the "metropolitan problem," and the significance of the growing federal-city relations for the states, particularly in respect of their role as partners in the federal system.

Local Government Organization. In 1962 the United States had a total of 91,236 governments, all but 51 of which were classed by the Census Bureau as local. This category included 3,043 counties, 17,997 municipalities, 17,144 townships, 34,678 school districts, and 18,323 special districts.[2] The national agencies administering the federal-city programs deal with any and all local governments, but local responsibilities usually fall on cities (municipalities) or special districts.

Ordinarily federal policy does not require a particular kind of government for local program administration. On the contrary, the law normally directs the federal agency to deal with any local unit—city, special district, (sometimes) county, or other—designated and given proper authorization by the state. Choice of the type of local organization therefore rests generally with the state or, by delegation, with the city. This is not true uniformly, for as many as one-fourth of all federal programs either favor or (in some instances) require the establishment of special units as agencies.

[2] U.S. Bureau of the Census, Census of Governments: 1962, vol. I, *Governmental Organization* (1963). The whole of this large volume deals with the subject of the number and organization of governments. The Introduction (pp. 1–26) will provide the casual reader with all he will wish to know about the subject; a table that appears on page 1 gives a summary of the number of governments by kinds, along with a ten-year trend, 1952–1962.

These variations in policy have resulted in a wide variety of local organizational forms. Sometimes the city, particularly the large city, exercises direct and continuing control over such programs as urban renewal, public housing, and airport development. Here the local public agency of urban renewal and the local housing authority of public housing are closely associated with (occasionally indeed operated as divisions of) traditional executive departments. Sometimes the LPA and the LHA will be joined as one, usually under the LHA rubric.[3] Such an arrangement offers no more than the usual hazards to program coordination or to comprehensive planning.

In many cases, however, there is an independent agency, often symbolized in a special district for the administration of one or another program. Sometimes there are constitutional limitations (on the tax rate or the incurring of debt, for example) which inhibit the city from assumption of full responsibility for a program. Occasionally it may be thought necessary to "remove a program from political control" by setting it apart from the city. Or it may be deemed advantageous to give a program separate status in order to direct special attention to it and to enlist citizen participation. Yet again an interest group may seize the initiative and force the creation of a special unit for a particular program. For these and like reasons special districts are increasing rapidly in number: from 1952 to 1962 the growth was approximately 50 per cent.

Most special district governments administer single functions, which vary widely in nature. Included are activities related to various aspects of education, fire protection, highways, health, hospitals, libraries, natural resources (drainage, flood control, irrigation, soil conservation, and so on), parks and recreation, sewage, cemeteries—the list is not complete, but it will serve to indicate the kinds of activities in which special districts engage. The whimsical nature of the state's decision to create or authorize special districts in this or that field is indicated by the facts that only two states have found it necessary to establish school building districts, and that

[3] The Advisory Commission on Intergovernmental Relations recently issued a report which on publication became the standard reference on this subject. See *Impact of Federal Urban Development Programs on Local Government Organization and Planning.* See p. 168, note 9, for full citation.

well over two-thirds of all such are found in Pennsylvania; that more than 60 per cent of all highway districts are in Missouri; and that New York has more than half of the health districts, Illinois more than half of the library districts, and Kansas almost half of the cemetery districts.

The foregoing list omits mention of the 1,099 housing and urban renewal districts which though scattered among thirty-six states and the District of Columbia are concentrated in four: Alabama, Georgia, Illinois, and Texas have almost 46 per cent of the total. In addition, there are seventy-six airport districts. The totals are not inclusive, but the figures nevertheless indicate wide use of the special district for the local administration of federal-city programs. It is worthy of emphasis that such districts are not merely appendages to the city but are governments in their own right; they are, as the census puts it, organized entities which possess governmental character and substantial autonomy.[4]

The widespread use of special districts reflects, among other things, single-minded pursuit of programmatic goals. Such single emphasis produces a number of side effects, by no means all of them benign. It serves to separate the program in question—urban renewal, public housing, and so on—from the mainstream of city affairs. By the same token it divorces the program from city politics, thereby denying it the juices of democracy. If, however, the purpose is to "remove the program from politics," then the special district does not necessarily achieve its end; for it may serve only to substitute for the general politics of the city the particular politics of a special clientele. This exchange is of dubious advantage, the more because special-district politics are less visible, less public, than general government politics. It can be argued persuasively that local school politics, for example, are as rough and tough and acrimonious as may be found anywhere.

Politics aside, special-district government means special-clientele and special-pleader government. On the one hand, the citizen who participates here has his interest and energy diverted from the affairs

[4] The kinds and numbers of special districts are summarized in Census of Governments, *op. cit.,* pp. 66–67. The census definition of a governmental unit appears on p. 15.

of the city; on the other hand, he is likely to become prisoner to a myopic commitment to what is after all a side show to the main performance. Citizens who interest themselves particularly in urban redevelopment are distinguished by higher economic status, those who participate actively in school affairs by higher education, from the politicians who run the city.[5] Dedication to an individual program by a vigorous, purposeful, and specialized clientele may have adverse results not alone for the city but for the program itself, as for example when the realtors seize control of the local public housing program. In such a case the housing authority may find itself in the hands of people who are in fact opposed to public housing. Now and again the governing board by positive action or by default delegates all substantial decision-making to the professional manager. This surrender, unhappily not uncommon, installs the bureaucrats in the seats of power; it represents the ultimate triumph of aseptic professionalism over politics. It may also mark the advent of utter irresponsibility.[6]

Finally, the promiscuous employment of special districts tends to atomize local government. The resulting fragmentation has serious implications for a concerted attack on local problems, for citizen concern in government, for the visibility of public activities, and for the responsibility of agencies and officials. A major casualty of the program-by-program approach to local government is planning, which becomes impossible in any meaningful sense when several governments in a locality share (or divide) responsibility for related public programs.

These criticisms of the special-district approach point to the desirability of integrating all program responsibilities in the local general government—that is, in the city. The argument is neither new nor universally persuasive, though its logic is hard to refute. Moreover, the advocates of integration are numerous and varied. Ten years ago Public Administration Service, in a report prepared

[5] Robert A. Dahl's analysis is suggestive on this point. See his *Who Governs?* (New Haven, Conn.: Yale University Press, 1961), especially pp. 176–178.

[6] This point of view is argued at length with respect to the public schools in Roscoe C. Martin, *Government and the Suburban School* (Syracuse, N.Y.: Syracuse University Press, 1962).

for the Commission on Intergovernmental Relations, concluded that "much of the strength [of the federal housing and urban redevelopment programs in Michigan] derives from the integration of municipal housing commissions into the general city governments."[7] A recent study noted, "The inability of many cities to harness into a common working pattern the local public agencies which handle segments of the relocation task in renewal has boded ill for the successful implementation of relocation,"[8] and argued for an integrated organizational structure as a means of combating tendencies toward atomization. And the Advisory Commission on Intergovernmental Relations, after discussing the issue with care, concluded that "general-purpose units of government should be favored as Federal aid recipients."[9] Not all knowledgeable observers would argue for universal reliance on the local general government; but few, apart from the staunch partisans commanded by individual programs, would support the special-district approach as a matter of principle.

It should be noted explicitly that the federal government bears a heavy responsibility for whatever shortcomings may have accrued from the use of special districts in the administration of federal-city programs. Special districts or authorities are favored over general governments for several programs; where this is not ostensibly the case, the permissive attitude on the part of the federal government encourages the states and communities to indulge their traditional predilection for fragmented government. Finally, fragmentation, lack of coordination, and emphasis on individual programs in Washington beget their counterpart sins at the local level. Federal organizational shortcomings, being more distant, are perhaps not so visible as those close to home, but they are there nevertheless for all who observe to see. What Washington might do to set its house in order is a matter for consideration elsewhere. In this immediate connection, the recommendation made by the ACIR is suggestive:

[7] Commission on Intergovernmental Relations, *Summaries of Survey Reports on the Administrative and Fiscal Impact of Federal Grants-in-Aid* (June 1955), p. 42.

[8] Henry W. Reynolds, Jr., "Local Government Structure in Urban Planning, Renewal, and Relocation," *Public Administration Review*, vol. XXIV, no. 1 (March 1964), pp. 14–20; quotation at p. 19.

[9] See the full quotation below which states ACIR's position.

The Commission recommends that the Congress and appropriate executive agencies take legislative and administrative action to remove from Federal aid programs for urban development all organizational limitations which require or promote special-purpose units of local government to the disadvantage of general-purpose units of local government (i.e., municipalities, towns, and counties). Other factors being equal, general-purpose units of government should be favored as Federal aid recipients. Special-purpose recipients should be required to coordinate their aided activities with general-purpose governments.[10]

The Metropolitan Problem. This problem may assume any of a number of forms depending on time, place, and circumstance, but depending most of all on the point of view of the observer. To some the problem resides in the disorderliness of the metropolitan governmental jungle, which obviously must be inefficient because it is untidy. Others, preoccupied with the success of this or that or the other program, identify the absence of an appropriate administrative agency as the central problem. Still others point to the ineffectiveness of the metropolitan area's machinery for decision-making, with respect, for example, to the allocation of resources.

For those whose primary interest is the federal-city grant-in-aid programs the problem resides in a harsh dilemma, which, only recently recognized as critical, remains largely unresolved. On the one hand, the problems that the federal-city programs were designed to cope with often are metropolitan in their scope, and in any case they are no respecters of local governmental entities. On the other hand, the federal agencies are directed to enter into agreements with local agencies designated or authorized by the state, and few of these in the past have paid much attention to metropolitan considerations. A complex network of local governments covers every square foot of the continent, sometimes several layers deep; but no more than a handful possess jurisdictions defined in metropolitan terms. In respect of federal grants-in-aid to the cities, the metropolitan problem lies in the noncongruity of local governments and metropolitan areas.

We have seen (in Chapter 1) something of the nature and extent of metropolitan growth: in 1960, 63 per cent of all Americans resided in 212 (continental) metropolitan areas which occupied

10 *Impact of Federal Urban Development Programs* . . ., *op. cit.*, p. 23.

only 10 per cent of the nation's area, and population increase from 1950 to 1960 was virtually limited to the larger cities and their environs. In 1962 the metropolitan areas contained 18,442 local governments. Of these, 6,004 were school districts, 5,411 were nonschool special districts, 4,142 were municipalities, and 310 were counties. That the metropolitan units were generally more populous than their counterparts outside the metropolitan areas is indicated by the fact that although 63 per cent of the total population lived in metropolitan areas, these contained only 20.2 per cent of all local governments. Metropolitan municipalities were 23 per cent of the total, special districts 29.5 per cent. Local governments in metropolitan areas are, however, increasing in number, those of greatest significance to the present inquiry quite rapidly. Thus municipalities increased 8 per cent from 1957 to 1962, special districts 45 per cent.

The special district, though by no means limited to the metropolitan area, is a peculiarly metropolitan phenomenon. Except for school districts (which are declining rapidly in number), special districts are the most numerous local governments found in metropolitan areas. Metropolitan area special districts constitute a larger percentage (29.5) of the national total than any other category of metropolitan governments. Housing and urban renewal districts are even more a characteristically metropolitan phenomenon: there were 391 such districts in metropolitan areas in 1962, and they comprised 36 per cent of all housing districts in the country.

In the present context, the metropolitan problem is conceptually quite simple, if seemingly beyond human ingenuity in solution. It inheres in the fact that the 212 metropolitan areas have not 212 governments but 87 times that number. The number varies from as few as half a dozen to more than a thousand: the Chicago metropolitan district in 1962 had 1,060 local governments. Eleven metropolitan areas with 250 or more governments each had all together 5,735 local governments. When the cutoff figure is reduced to 200 local governments, 24 metropolitan areas qualified for membership in this unenviably exclusive club in 1962. The problem is that of bringing action programs to bear on metropolitan areas which have not one government but many.[11]

[11] Census of Governments, *op. cit.*, pp. 10–12. The pages cited contain

The metropolitan problem as identified here may be attacked in any of several ways. The county offers a promising approach toward alleviation of the problem, particularly because it is the only local general government of broad geographic reach, and more particularly yet because 133 metropolitan areas lie wholly within the confines of individual counties. So far, so good—but what of the 79 metropolitan areas which spread into two or more counties; and, more vexing yet, what of the 24 areas which are interstate? The county has utility in respect of the metropolitan problem, but clearly it is limited. Again, metropolitan pressure with respect to a particular problem can be alleviated through creation of a special district covering the problem area. Wide use is made of the special-district device for dealing with individual (sometimes it is two or three) metropolitan problems. Yet again, a measure of reason can be introduced by voluntary cooperation among the governments of a metropolitan area, as through support of an areawide council of governments or a metropolitan planning commission. At least a dozen additional arrangements exist for the alleviation of the metropolitan problem in one or another of its various guises, but it cannot be truly said that a satisfactory solution to the problem has been achieved in more than a very small number of instances.[12] And even these solutions in all likelihood will prove in the end to have been temporary.

A constructive approach to the metropolitan problem within the framework of federal-city relations will require positive action by all governments involved. It is not realistic to expect much more than patchwork action by local governments, since any vigorous

---

tables on which the above summary is based. The volume also contains detailed tables on local governments in metropolitan areas.

[12] There is an increasing flood of literature on the metropolis and its problems. Citations of use in the current context would include Roscoe C. Martin, *Metropolis in Transition: Local Government Adaptation to Changing Urban Needs* (Washington, D.C.: Housing and Home Finance Agency, September 1963); Advisory Commission on Intergovernmental Relations, *Alternative Approaches to Intergovernmental Reorganization in Metropolitan Areas* (June 1962); and *Governmental Structure, Organization, and Planning in Metropolitan Areas: Suggested Action by Local, State, and National Governments*, A Report by the Advisory Commission on Intergovernmental Relations (Printed for the Use of the Committee on Government Operations, House of Representatives, 87th Congress, 1st Session, July 1961).

move in the direction of metropolitan government would of necessity have adverse effects on some local entities. The states for the most part have remained lethargic in reacting to the metropolitan challenge, though a few have bestirred themselves—not very vigorously in most instances—since the late 1950s. As late as 1960 most federal agencies remained oblivious of the metropolitan area, dealing with the city or other local unit as though municipal action were adequate to metropolitan needs. Since that time there has been an increasing awareness that the problems to which the grant-in-aid programs are addressed are substantially beyond both the resources and the legal jurisdictions of existing local governments. In the mid-1960s there is considerable interest in and emphasis on metropolitan planning, with the ACIR beating the drum for planning and the federal agencies falling into step one by one. It is not necessary to conclude that this emphasis is really bad because experience warrants the judgment that it is not really good. Where there is no cure, a palliative must be employed. But more powerful medicine than planning is required to bring the grant-in-aid programs effectively to grips with metropolitan problems. A prescription that carries promise of truly significant result remains to be written.

The Expanded Partnership and the States. The third problem to be considered here concerns the effect that expansion of the federal system has had on the states. Two convictions are widely held and frequently voiced: the first, that the states are losing ground as members of the federal partnership; the second, that grants-in-aid, and more particularly the grants made direct by the federal government to the cities, are responsible for this trend. Leonard D. White expressed this view in 1953 when he prophesied gloomily that "if the present trends continue for another quarter century, the states may be left hollow shells, operating primarily as the field districts of Federal departments and dependent upon the Federal treasury for their support."[13] Others take the contrary position that the states have nothing to fear from the new federalism, that they are, in fact, in sound condition. Among these is former President Harry

[13] Leonard D. White, *The States and the Nation* (Baton Rouge, La.: Louisiana State University Press, 1953), p. 3.

Truman who, when confronted with Professor White's view, commented, "I am of the opinion most of these professional political scientists know very little about government as it is operated, . . . I think he is wrong about the States becoming a shell."[14] Two years after White uttered his lugubrious prophecy, Professor William Anderson commented in this vein: "The idea that the states have declined in importance and are declining, I think, is unsupported by the weight of evidence. . . . It seems to me the states never were in history any stronger, any freer, any more active than they are today."[15] Where between the opposing views of White and Anderson, both experienced and highly regarded students of American government, lies "the weight of evidence"? What are the facts?

An anterior question concerns the kinds of facts admissible. A variety of criteria might be invoked in assessing a government's health: scope of activities pursued, degree of citizen participation and support, resources commanded, credit rating (ability to incur debt)—these suggest themselves at once, though it should be added quickly that not all observers would apply these and like criteria in the same way or to the same purpose. It is not our present intention to appraise the soundness of state government; that has been done, at least in a general way, in Chapter 3. The purpose here is less ambitious; it is simply to determine whether the states are in fact withering away, whether they seem to be in danger of becoming "hollow shells." This may be done by comparing the growth of state government with the growth of national and city governments.

One indicator of governmental growth or decadence is provided by revenue trends. The latest figures available at the time of writing revealed that during the five-year period 1960–1964 total state tax collections increased 33 per cent. Income (individual and corporation) taxes increased almost 50 per cent. Collections from every individual tax experienced substantial growth during the period, and almost every one yielded an increase from year to

[14] Hearings before a Subcommittee of the Committee on Government Operations, House of Representatives, 85th Congress, 1st Session, *Federal-State-Local Relations, State and Local Officials,* Part 2 (1958), p. 641.

[15] Arthur W. Macmahon (ed.), *Federalism Mature and Emergent* (New York: Doubleday and Co., 1955), p. 26.

186 The Cities and the Federal System

year.[16] This does not sound like the death rattle of moribund government. It excites curiosity concerning the trends to be disclosed by comparisons.

From 1902 to 1962 the federal government's general revenues increased 141 times, the general revenues of local governments 45 times. During the same period the general revenues of the states multiplied 164 times. If taxes alone are considered, the growth figures are as follows: for the federal government, 126 times; for local governments, 33 times; for the states, 132 times. It is true that the states departed from a much smaller revenue base in 1902 than did the other two levels of government. It is also true that in 1962 the states still collected fewer dollars than either the national government or the localities. For present purposes, however, what is significant is not actual dollars but *trends in revenue collections.* Whether computed in terms of general revenues or in terms of taxes alone, *the revenue growth rate of state government over six decades is greater than that of either of the other levels.*

The figures for expenditures corroborate the trend established by analysis of revenues. The direct expenditures (this category excludes intergovernmental expenditures) of the federal government increased 187 times from 1902 to 1962, those of local governments 47 times. Direct expenditures by state governments increased 187 times during the six decades, but if the computation is carried further it is seen that the growth of direct expenditures by the states exceeded that of the federal government, though by a narrow margin. If, however, war and war-related costs are excluded and the figures are limited to domestic expenditures, then the direct expenditures of state governments grew more rapidly from 1902 to 1962 than those of either the national government or the communities.

The data on indebtedness tell the same story. The federal debt is greater than that of state and local governments combined, as every schoolboy knows through constant iteration; but from 1952 to 1962 the federal debt increased only a little more than 11 per cent,

[16] U.S. Bureau of the Census, "State Tax Collections in 1964" (G-SF64-No. 3, October 1964), Table 1, p. 4.

that of local governments and that of the states 250 and 320 per cent respectively. It is worthy of emphasis that the total state debt increased more than three times from 1952 to 1962. Some would say—indeed many have said—that this figure reflects an unsound condition in the states. The truth is that, within limits not yet begun to be approached, a growing debt betokens an active and expanding government. That concept aside, state indebtedness is growing considerably faster than that of either federal or local government.[17]

Further corroborative evidence is provided by analysis of the data available for public employment and payrolls. From October 1946 to October 1962 federal civilian employees increased 4.3 per cent; in these sixteen years the employees of local governments increased 87 per cent, those of state governments 209 per cent. During the same period federal civilian monthly payrolls expanded 235.6 per cent and those of local governments 435.2 per cent. At the same time, state payrolls were increasing almost 496 per cent.[18]

By several criteria, therefore, the states have grown faster since 1902, and more especially in recent years, than either of the other levels of government. In revenues collected, in expenditures, in indebtedness, in number of employees and salaries and wages paid them, state government is expanding rapidly. The data examined tell nothing about the internal soundness or the present position of the states, but treat only of comparative growth among the three levels of government. They demonstrate conclusively that the states are growing more rapidly than either the national government or the cities.

This phenomenon has not escaped the attention of others. Alan Campbell, appraising state and local government contributions to the national economy, concluded that "the rate of growth in expenditures, revenues and employment by state and local governments outstrips the growth rate of all other parts of the economy,

17 The computations on which the above generalizations rest depend upon statistics drawn from U.S. Bureau of the Census, *Census of Governments: 1962*, vol. VI, no. 4, *Historical Statistics on Governmental Finances and Employment* (1964), Tables 3, 5, and 6.

18 *Census of Governments: 1962*, vol. III, *Compendium of Public Employment* (1963), Table 2.

public or private."[19] Frederick C. Mosher and Orville F. Poland have written to the same general effect. A major conclusion of their study is that "the role of the federal government in direct domestic expenditures unrelated to defense, vis-à-vis other governments, has been slightly declining."[20]

Are the states in fact declining in influence and significance as partners in the federal system? The evidence examined suggests the contrary. At the beginning of the twentieth century they were in a very poor position: they raised and spent comparatively little money, employed few people, pursued a limited range of activities. They were oriented toward the facilitation of public action rather than toward action itself; they passed enabling legislation and rendered whatever assistance was convenient, but the tasks of government (in the sense of service) fell largely to the cities. The states were in fact not much disposed toward positive government in 1900. In the last few decades they have begun to assert themselves, with a resulting growth which, compared with that of other governments, has been quite rapid.

As partners in the federal system, the states in a sense perform a broker or middleman function, and this is true particularly with respect to the grant-in-aid system. In 1962 almost 23 per cent of all state general revenues came in the form of payments from the federal government, and almost 35 per cent of all state general expenditures went to local governments in the form of "state aid."[21] Some see in these facts danger that the states will lose their vitality and become, as Leonard White prophesied, "hollow shells" serving simply as way stations on the road from Washington to the city halls or the reverse. The advocates of states' rights are particularly vigorous in their denunciation of the programs which involve direct federal-city relations. On the broad subject of grants-in-aid, Frederick C. Mosher has made a comment that is as relevant to the federal-city aid programs as it is to the entire system. It is worth quoting at length:

[19] Alan K. Campbell, "Most Dynamic Sector," *National Civic Review*, vol. LIII, no. 2 (February 1964), pp. 74–82; quotation at p. 74.
[20] Frederick C. Mosher and Orville F. Poland, *The Costs of American Governments: Facts, Trends, Myths* (New York: Dodd, Mead & Co., 1964), p. 48.
[21] *Historical Statistics, op. cit.,* Tables 8 and 9.

Grants-in-aid . . . have been advocated on a variety of grounds: equalization of service; equalization of tax burden; improvement and maintenance of standards of service; stimulation of new activities. Seldom has it been made explicit that grants, looked upon in their aggregate amounts, are a device whereby the superior revenue capabilities of a higher level of government may be made available to support, in part, the activity responsibilities of a lower level. They have made it possible to provide services and standards of service that many or most or even all lower levels could not or would not support from their own resources. And while many decry grants as a device for centralizing control over activities that have been, or should be, conducted at a lower level, their real effect, in the larger sense, may be just the opposite. They make it possible to maintain the activities themselves and the operating responsibility for them at the lower level—activities which otherwise might be foregone, or be conducted at minimal levels of service, or be taken over by higher levels. Viewed in this light, grants-in-aid may well be the principal instrument whereby our system of government remains, for internal purposes, the most decentralized of all the governments of the large and modern countries of the world. The centralizing factors, which cannot be handled through grants-in-aid, are wars and the fear of war.[22]

THE EXPANDED PARTNERSHIP AND DEMOCRATIC GOVERNMENT

It is a basic American tradition that the most democratic government is the one closest to the people. The prototype of American democracy is the New England town; the principal current practitioners, in fancy, are the town, the midwestern village, the small school district—in short, little governments everywhere. In the eyes of those who hold this position, any government whose center is more than a stone's throw away is a "big" government, and therefore not to be trusted. This doctrine accounts in good part for rural distrust of the city, and for the persistence of the agrarian state of mind when the conditions that fathered it and indeed when rural life itself have all but disappeared.

It is not difficult to demonstrate that much of what passes for democratic government in the very small units is neither democratic

[22] Frederick C. Mosher, *Recent Trends in Governmental Finances in the United States* (Berkeley, Calif.: Bureau of Public Administration, University of California, May 1961), p. 33.

nor, in any significant sense, government. It is not democratic because control by the people often is illusory; individuals, families, or corporations make decisions in the name of the electorate, and the organs of government operate in the absence of effective popular responsibility. It is scarcely worthy to be called government because the functions to be discharged are so picayune and the resources available for their support so minuscule as to beggar the concept of public action. There is abundant reason to question the colonial tradition of government by friends and neighbors as it finds application in twentieth-century America.[23]

Moving the argument up one level, the states' rights position is in the tradition of little government, with adjustments for scope and size. It is true that the states, occupying as they do a middle position, are subjected to criticism from both bottom and top. From below they appear to be major agents of centralization, and are often denounced as such. From another point of view, however, the states may properly be judged by their contributions toward solution of the total problem of government. It is primarily as partners in the federal system that the states make such contributions, and it is here that they assert the doctrine of states' rights. "Bring government back home" and "Return government to the people" are battle cries equally familiar in the cause of local autonomy and in that of states' rights. In both cases the plea is for more government close by, less government far away; more little government, less big government; more personal government, less anonymous government. In point of fact it is quite clear that the goal sought often is not local autonomy or states' rights as such but rather *less government,* and moreover government more immediately and more directly subject to control. When the power company of a large northeastern state becomes a vigorous supporter of states' rights, one may be permitted to wonder whose interests are involved and how they are expected to be served.

The state described in Chapter 3 would scarcely be considered a serious candidate for high honors when judged by democratic criteria. Its government is too often far removed from the people it purports to serve, in terms of both popular participation and public

[23] This theme is developed at length in Roscoe C. Martin, *Grass Roots* (University, Alabama: University of Alabama Press, 1957).

accountability. The unrepresentative legislative body is only one evidence, albeit the most flagrant one, of the flouting of popular sovereignty by the states. The failure of most states to recognize the problems of urban America and take positive action regarding them, their inability to organize for effective administration, their addiction to traditional ways in the face of palpable need for dramatic new public programs, the limited views held by their leaders of proper public responsibilities—these shortcomings among others demonstrate the present inability of the states to function in accordance with the standards of democratic government.

There are nonfederal entities that are democratic in organization and in the conduct of their affairs. These are the cities and in less (but growing) degree the urban counties. The cities are in the mainstream of twentieth-century government. The massive problems that characterize an urban-industrial society center on the cities, which must play a basic role in any serious effort to deal with those problems. The cities are acutely aware through harsh experience of the disjunctions of urban life, and are committed to their alleviation as a condition of survival. The cities are, moreover, dedicated to both the principle and the practice of democratic government. Municipal governments are in truth "close to the people," not as close as the town governments of New England are reputed to have been, but as close as the scale and complexity of modern life will allow. This closeness manifests itself at every stage of the governmental process; more particularly it is seen in the vitality of city elections and in the many means through which municipal officials are held accountable for their actions. All this is not to say that urban government is without fault, or that it is not susceptible of improvement. Notwithstanding its shortcomings, however, it remains true as a rule that government at the urban level—that of the cities generally, that of the urbanized counties increasingly—is the most effective, in terms of both democratic controls and performance, to be found this side of Washington.

It may be argued persuasively that the national government is more sensitive to public needs in the beginning and more subject to popular control in the end than are either state or local governments. There is advantage in separation from the immediate scene of action: from personal acquaintance with families adversely affected by the closing of a military establishment, from daily contact with constituents, from friendly association with the officers of corporations—in short, from closeness to individual people. Modern government must of necessity be government for the people as a mass, so far at least as the setting of major policies is concerned. For the setting and indeed for the execution of high policy, general grasp and perspective are infinitely more important than emotional involvement with or personal commitment to individual citizens in particular.

This line of reasoning leads to the conclusion that the most democratic government *in* the United States is in fact the government *of* the United States. The most democratic legislative body in the country is the United States Senate, whose members represent the largest and most highly generalized constituencies. After the Senate comes the House of Representatives, and for the same reason as before: congressional districts are second only to the states (U.S. senatorial districts) themselves in the size and generalness of their voting constituencies. And in terms both of pure doctrine and of practice, the President is the most democratic single official in all American government; he alone is elected by vote of all the people, and he alone is in a position to see the wants and needs and to appraise the hopes and aspirations of all Americans. At a lower level of abstraction, federal administrators are in their way equally democratic. They are charged with the execution of national programs democratically conceived and defined, and are held responsible in a variety of ways for the proper discharge of their obligations.

The open marriage of the federal government and the cities cannot but have strengthened American democracy. It has brought into close collaboration the two most democratic of governments in a way that has resulted in the invigoration of both, but especially of the city. On the one hand, "centralization" turns out on examination to be more a war cry of embattled local interests than a trend; but on the other hand true centralization, if it should come to exist, would represent a trend in power and influence from generally less democratic governments toward a generally more democratic government, from bewildered state and local governments toward a government with some sense of national urgency and mission. What is important, however, is not federal centralization, whether as threat or as specter, but that the resources of the nation have been brought to bear on problems previously considered local—and previously largely ignored. That this has been accomplished without threat to democracy or harm to the federal system is a tribute to the toughness and flexibility of the American way of government.

Index

New York City: growth of, 2–3; politics of, 31; assessed property value, 33; percentage of state population, 33; public employment, 34; and reapportionment, 57; Airports Service Regional Office, 116

New York State, 33; constitution of, 50–1; and apportionment, 55, 58; agencies, 61; intergovernmental expenditures, 74; Office of Local Government, 76; and urban renewal, 127; and public housing, 132; special districts, 178

Nicholson, W. F., Mayor, and airport development, 150

Norfolk, Virginia, 39; urban renewal, 149; Norfolk Redevelopment and Housing Authority, 157–8; airport development, 161–2

North Carolina: early cooperative arrangements, 39; Association of County Commissioners, 165

Open space program, 132

Pennsylvania: growth of Philadelphia, 2–3; intergovernmental expenditures, 74; views on airport development, 95; appropriation for airports, 98; public housing, 132; special districts, 178

Planning, urban renewal programs, 152; interest in, 184

Poland, Orville F.: on growth of governments, 188; *The Costs of American Governments*, 188n

Pollution: problem in urban areas, 16; abatement and state interest, 75, 166; as national problem, 172; control, 174

Presidency: and federalism, 26–7, 41; and federal-aid for airports, 86, 89

Public Administration Service, 178–80

Public Housing, Low-Rent, 34; contribution of states, 75; federal grants, 114, 115; as result of depression, 128; Housing Acts, 128; U.S. Housing Authority, 128; local housing authority, 129–30; current projects, 131; features of, 131; federal contribution, 140; state interest in, 166, 174

Public Housing Administration: relocation of families, 125n; regional offices, 130; characteristics

of, 142–3; and delays in programs, 156–7; auditing procedures, 157–8

Puerto Rico, 41; grants for airport development, 121; public housing, 131

Quesada, E. R., General, 160

Reapportionment, legislative, 31; Supreme Court interest in, 52n; reactions of states to, 79

Reorganization, state, 63–6

Revenue trends, government, 185–6

Reynolds, Henry W., Jr., "Local Government Structure in Urban Planning, Renewal, and Relocation," 180n

Reynolds v. Sims, 55n

Rich, Bennett M., *State Constitutions: The Governor*, 64n

Rockefeller, Nelson, 77

Roman v. Sincock, 55n

Roosevelt, Franklin D., 26, 27, 111

Saltonstall, Leverett, Senator, 101, 103

Schmeckebier, Laurence F., *The Aeronautics Branch, Department of Commerce . . .* , 84n

Senate, U.S.: airport construction, 88; supports states' rights views, 101; Committee on Interstate Commerce, *Civil Aviation and Air Transport*, 84n, hearings on federal-state vs. federal-city relations, 102; Subcommittee on Aviation of Committee on Commerce, 93, 94, testimony of American Municipal Association, 97

Slayton, William L., on trends in urban renewal, 122n, 125n

Slum Clearance and Urban Renewal Program, 115

Special Districts, 177–80, 182

State aid, 72–4

State-city conflict, 94

State governments: traditional responsibility for cities, 18; failure to assume responsibilities, 46–7; constitutions of, 47, 48–51; agricultural interests in constitutions, 48; amending process, 49; agencies, 61; evolution of system of administration, 61–3; office of governor, 62, 64; movement for reorganization, 63–6; revenue, 67–72, 164–6, 185–6; expenditures,

AMERICAN FEDERALISM
The Urban Dimension

An Arno Press Collection

Atkinson, Raymond C. **The Federal Role in Unemployment Compensation Administration.** 1941

Benson, George C. S. **The New Centralization.** 1941

Betters, Paul V. **Cities and the 1936 Congress** *and* **Recent Federal-City Relations** with J. Kerwin Williams and Sherwood L. Reeder. 1936

Betters, Paul V. **Federal Services to Municipal Governments.** 1931

Civil Aeronautics Authority. **Airport Survey.** 1939

Colean, Miles L. **Housing for Defense.** 1940

Connery, Robert H. and Richard H. Leach. **The Federal Government and Metropolitan Areas.** 1960

The Council of State Governments. **Federal Grants-In-Aid.** 1949

The Council of State Governments. **Federal-State Relations.** 1949

Dearing, Charles L. **American Highway Policy.** 1941

Federal Aid to the Cities. 1977

Federal-City Relations in the 1930s. 1977

Friedman, Lawrence M. **Government and Slum Housing.** 1968

Graves, W. Brooke, editor. **Intergovernmental Relations in the United States.** 1940

Heer, Clarence. **Federal Aid and the Tax Problem.** 1939

Keith, John A. H. and William C. Bagley. **The Nation and the Schools.** 1920

Lutz, Edward A. **Some Problems and Alternatives in Developing Federal Block Grants to States for Public Welfare Purposes.** 1954

MacDonald, Austin F. **Federal Aid:** A Study of the American Subsidy System. 1928

Martin, Roscoe C. **The Cities and the Federal System.** 1965

Millett, John D. **The Works Progress Administration in New York City.** 1938

Reynolds, Harry. W., Jr., editor. **Intergovernmental Relations in the United States.** 1965

Tax Policy League. **Tax Relations Among Governmental Units.** 1938

Thompson, Walter. **Federal Centralization.** 1923

Tobey, James A. **The National Government and Public Health.** 1926

U.S. Advisory Commission on Intergovernmental Relations. **Metropolitan America.** 1966

U.S. Advisory Commission on Intergovernmental Relations. **The Role of Equalization in Federal Grants.** 1964

U.S. Commission on Intergovernmental Relations. **A Report to the President for Transmittal to the Congress.** 1955

U.S. House Committee on Banking and Currency. **Demonstration Cities, Housing and Urban Development, and Urban Mass Transit.** 1966. Two Vols. in One.

U.S. House Committee on Banking, Currency and Housing. **The New York City Fiscal Crisis:** Selections from *Debt Financing Problems of State and Local Government.* 1975

U.S. House Committee on Government Operations. **Federal-State-Local Relations: Federal Grants-In-Aid** *and* **Federal-State-Local Relations: State and Local Officials.** 1958/1959. Two Vols. in One.

U.S. National Resources Committee, Research Committee on Urbanism. **Interim Report to the National Resources Committee.** 1936

U.S. National Resources Committee. **Urban Government.** 1939

U.S. Senate Committee on Government Operations. **Creative Federalism.** 1967. Three Vols. in One

U.S. Senate Committee on Government Operations. **The Effect of Inflation and Recession on State and Local Governments.** 1975

U.S. Senate Select Committee on Reconstruction and Production. **The Federal Government and the Housing Problem:** Selections from *Reconstruction and Production.* 1921. Two Vols.

U.S. Treasury Department, The Committee on Intergovernmental Fiscal Relations. **Federal, State, and Local Government Fiscal Relations.** 1943

Warren, Charles. **Congress as Santa Claus.** 1932